A Complete PMBOK 6th Edition Practice Exam – Project Management Fundamentals

Dr. Renay Carver, PhD, PMP, CISM, CRISC, CSM, CSP, SAFe[4.5]

INTRODUCTION

Thank you for purchasing this practice exam. I hope you will find it to be a valuable resource in your preparation for the PMP certification exam. The content of this book is based upon PMBOK 6TH edition, which is the latest blueprint covering the following project management fundamentals:

- 10 Project Management Knowledge Areas
- 5 Project Management Process Groups
- 47 Project Management Processes
- Agile Project Management
- Professional and Social Responsibility of Project Managers

ABOUT THIS DOCUMENT

This book contains a full PMBOK 6th edition practice test, designed to provide you with the necessary practice experience to prepare yourself for the actual exam. There are 200 questions, some of which are based on cases that are provided with the questions. These questions are modeled after the kind of delicate or complex phrasing you will encounter when attempting the actual exam. After diligently using this book as intended, and when using the book in combination with your regular project management study material, you should improve your understanding of project management fundamental practices. The topics and types of questions in this practice exam are offered in a manner to resemble the actual PMBOK 6th edition exam.

The first part of this book contains the practice exam, and the second part references the answer key. Additionally, the answer key contains the correct answer and the information which will lead you to the correct answer. The brief explanations direct you to the appropriate reference source to help you understand how to choose the best answer.

HOW TO TAKE THIS PRACTICE EXAM:

This exam contains 200 questions in this practice test, for which you can take 4 hours. You will need to answer at least 137 questions correctly in order to score sufficiently at a level which will indicate your preparedness to earn a passing score on the PMP certification exam. In taking the practice test, you may wish to mimic the environment in which you will take the actual exam. Set the timer for 4 hours. Use pen and paper and take your time in reviewing the questions and related answers. If you do not know the answer, you may wish to skip the response. Write a question mark adjacent to the unanswered question, so you can flag the answer for later review, and return to the question after you have finished answering the remaining questions. Do not waste time if you are stuck! Allow sufficient time to return to unanswered questions and to review your answers. Remember, it is important to understand the logic behind the questions and answers.

Good Luck!

Best Regards,

Dr. Renay Carver, PhD, PMP, CISM, CRISC, CSM, CSP, SAFe$^{4.5}$

This page intentionally left blank

1.

You are the project manager of USFL project for ABC Bank, and are leading an 18-month initiative to enhance business and sales practices. The project entails the use of cutting edge analytics and technology that will impact compliance reporting. You discover a new regulation may be established, in 12 months, and such regulation may result in additional project cost. Although the regulatory agency has not confirmed the date of enforcement, as the project manager, you notate the risk on the risk register. The risk associated with the uncertainty of the future regulatory event is an example of what type of risk? *Select the best answer.*

   a.   Variability Risk
   b.   Inherent Risk
   c.   Residual Risk
   d.   Ambiguity Risk

2.

As the project manager for Opti-Tech, you have been assigned to lead a team through the development of a software application that will improve organizational processes. The 9-month project entails data migration to a cloud-based solution, hosted by a third party. Since the organization has been hampered in the past by poor data quality, you have decided to meet with the data owners every 2 weeks, after each incremental migration, to evaluate data migrated to date. These meetings, which will facilitate the team's identification of data source changes more frequently, are an example of what agile custom? *Select the best answer.*

   a.   Iteration reviews
   b.   Short feedback loops
   c.   Quality assurance
   d.   Tollgate reviews

3.

Agile processes promote _______________. The sponsors, developers, and users should be able to maintain a constant pace indefinitely. *Fill in the blank.*
   a.   continuous development
   b.   sustainable development
   c.   continuous delivery
   d.   sustainable delivery

4.

You have been assigned as the Project Manager for an agile project that involves development of a new proprietary customer relationship management system. The application will enable your company to be more competitive in the market. After reviewing the business and system requirements with the project team, you realize the large project scope may be hindered by a complex design and a cumbersome approach to delivery due to multiple overlaps and dependencies. Which of the following actions should you do to help deliver an agile project that meets stakeholder needs? *Select the best answer.*

a. Divide the project into several releases, which will accommodate design complexity and allow stakeholders an opportunity to offer faster feedback
b. Lengthen the project schedule, since based upon your experience, the timeline will be extended anyway due to the design complexity
c. Keep the project schedule as-is, and request the business remove gold-plated, nice to have requirements as soon as possible
d. Advise the team to decide the schedule outcome, because your self-organized team makes the best decisions!

5.

Build projects around ________________ individuals. Give them the ____________ and support they need, and trust them to get the job done. ***Fill in the blank.***
   a. motivated, tools
   b. competent, tools
   c. motivated, environment
   d. competent, resources

6.

Which of the following is not true about agile / adaptive environments? ***Select the best answer.***

   a. High-variability environments incur more uncertainty and risk
   b. High-variability environments incur less uncertainty and risk
   c. High-variability environments incur moderate uncertainty and risk
   d. High-variability environments have no risk

7.

You work as a project manager for SoftTech Inc., and you are tasked with leading an agile team. Which one of the following answers is not an attribute of an agile team? ***Select the best answer.***

   a. Stable work environment
   b. Dedicated people
   c. Cross-functional team members
   d. High uncertainty/high change

8.

Agile and the Kanban Method are descendants of _________________. ***Fill in the blank.***

   a. Waterfall
   b. Lean Thinking
   c. Scrumban
   d. Mini-waterfall

9.

When teams deliver small increments, they are better able to understand the true customer requirements and more accurately than with a static written specification. ***Select the best answer.***

   a. True

b. False

10.

As the _________________ in the project increases, the likelihood of changes, wasted work, and rework also increases, which is costly and time consuming. ***Fill in the blank.***

a. Risk
b. Number of Resources
c. Uncertainty
d. Number of Stakeholders

11.

You work as a project manager for SoftTech Inc., and you are tasked with defining how to conduct risk management activities for the project. What is the name of the process which you are leading? ***Select the best answer.***

a. Plan Risk Response
b. Plan Risk Management
c. Plan Risk Identification
d. Perform Qualitative Risk Analysis

12.

Which of the following elements is not included in the Risk Management Plan? ***Select the best answer.***

a. Funding
b. Timing
c. Roles and Responsibilities
d. Resource Requirements

13.

You work as a project manager for Bubbles Tech, Inc., and are leading a cross-functional team to manufacture smartphone audio accessories. Your Engineering department stakeholder escalated a risk regarding a key vendor's delayed timeframe for delivering an input component. The component may be delivered 2 weeks after the original delivery date, adding to overall project risk. What is the document where you will add the vendor risk, indicating important drivers of the overall project risk exposure and summarizing information on identified individual project risks? ***Select the best answer.***

a. Business Charter
b. Risk Report
c. Project Plan
d. Risk Register

14.

After completing the Plan Risk Management process early in the project, the project manager no longer needs to revisit the process, as identified risks have already been documented in the Risk Register. Choose the correct answer. ***Select the best answer.***

a. True

b. False

According to the Uncertainty and Complexity Model (inspired by the Stacey Complexity Model), projects with high uncertainty in requirements and technical degree are _____________. *Fill in the blank.*

a. Chaos (fundamentally risky)
b. Chaos (fundamentally simple)
c. Complex (fundamentally risk)
d. Complex (fundamentally simple)

You work as a project manager for Do Re Mi, Inc., and are leading a cross-functional team to update the organization's human capital application systems. Given the project characteristics, you decide to follow a traditional life cycle approach, with the bulk of the planning made upfront and deliverables completed sequentially. What life cycle approach does your team follow? *Select the best answer.*

a. Predictive life cycle
b. Iterative life cycle
c. Waterfall life cycle
d. Agile life cycle

You work as a project manager for Fa So La, Inc., and are leading a cross-functional team to update the organization's Legal / Compliance application systems. Given the project characteristics, your team agrees business customers may share feedback for unfinished work, so that improvements and modifications can be made during project execution. What type of life cycle approach does your team follow? *Select the best answer.*

a. Waterfall life cycle
b. Iterative life cycle
c. Incremental life cycle
d. Agile life cycle

You work as a project manager for Musical Notes, Inc., and are leading a cross-functional team to update the organization's Finance (reporting & analytics) application systems. Given the project characteristics, your team and the business customer agree finished deliverables will be provided to the business customers immediately for use, even though full functionality has not yet been achieved. What type of life cycle approach does your team follow? *Select the best answer.*

a. Predictive life cycle
b. Iterative life cycle
c. Incremental life cycle
d. Agile life cycle

You work as a project manager for Do Re Me, Inc., and are leading a cross-functional team to update the Marketing department's lead generation software application. Given the project characteristics, your team agrees business customers may share feedback for unfinished work and provide finished deliverables to the business customers immediately for use. What type of life cycle approach does your team follow? *Select the best answer.*

    a. Iterative life cycle
    b. Incremental life cycle
    c. Predictive life cycle
    d. Agile life cycle

20.

Plan-driven, non-agile approaches opposite of Agile on the project approach continuum are typically referred to as _____________________. *Fill in the blank.*

    a. Waterfall
    b. Serial
    c. Incremental
    d. Predictive

21.

Predictive projects typically deliver value at the ______________ of the project. *Fill in the blank.*

    a. End
    b. Beginning
    c. Middle
    d. Neither A, B, or C, as predictive projects rarely deliver value, according to agile

22.

Agile projects do not utilize planning, as the project teams are self-organizing, which negates the need for stringent planning. *Select the best answer.*

    a. True
    b. False

23.

The figure below is indicative of which project life cycle approach. *Select the best answer.*

    a. Predictive life cycle
    b. Iterative life cycle
    c. Agile life cycle
    d. Incremental life cycle

24.

In the Incremental life cycle approach, project teams follow defined activities to deliver a subset of the product solution. Which of the following is the correct, iterative approach for incremental life cycle projects? *Select the best answer.*

a. Analyze, Design, Build, Test, Deliver
b. Analyze, Develop, Build, Test, Deploy
c. Analyze, Design, Construct, Test, Deploy
d. Define, Design, Build, Test, Deploy

25.

In Flow-Based agile, the time it takes to complete a feature is not the same for each feature. *Select the best answer.*

a. True
b. False

26.

The diagram below is an example of _______________ approach. *Select the best answer.*

a. Flow-Based Agile
b. Iteration-Based Agile
c. Incremental-Based Agile
d. Waterfall

27.

You work as a project manager for Do Re Me, Inc., and are leading a cross-functional team to implement a new applicant tracking system. Requirements, Analysis, Design, Build, and Test activities are all performed in a single iteration, with value delivered incrementally. This approach is an example of what type of life cycle approach? *Select the best answer.*

a. Predictive life cycle
b. Agile/Iteration-Based life cycle
c. Dynamic life cycle
d. Incremental life cycle

28.

You work as a project manager for Blue Moon, Inc., and are leading a cross-functional team to implement a new robo-advisor platform. Requirements, Analysis, Design, Build, and Test activities are all performed in a single iteration, however the time it takes to complete the features results in one iterative cycle extending longer than the previous cycle. This approach is an example of what type of approach? *Select the best answer.*

a. Waterfall
b. Flow-Based Agile
c. Rational Unified Process
d. Software design

29.

Which of the following project approaches considers the time it takes to complete a feature is not the same for each feature? *Select the best answer.*

a. Waterfall life cycle

b. Rational Unified Process
c. Software design
d. Flow-Based Agile

30.

Which of the following project approaches recognizes each timebox is the same size, and concludes in working tested features? *Select the best answer.*

a. Rational Unified Process
b. Iteration-Based Agile
c. Scrumban
d. Flow-Based Agile

31.

Which one of the following is an example activity employed by project teams to reduce waste and rework in an agile project? *Select the best answer.*

a. Keep prioritization of requirements according to the original scope, as changes may result in scope creep
b. Incorporate short feedback loops, to gather stakeholder commentary on a more frequent basis
c. Leave the process unchanged, as waste is expected in the development cycle
d. Extend the feedback loops, to allow more stakeholders time to opine on product delivery

32.

Assigned as a project manager for Turtles Delux, Inc., Brad notices the development team continues to deliver product requiring significant rework each iterative cycle. What activity should Brad recommend the project team follow to eliminate waste? *Select the best answer.*

a. Leave the process unchanged, as waste is expected in the development cycle
b. Keep prioritization of requirements according to the original scope, as changes may result in scope creep
c. Frequently adapt the process, to stay nimble and focused as determined necessary by the self-organized team
d. Continue to deliver value only at the major milestones, as phase-gates are the optimal time for stakeholders to evaluate product updates

33.

Which one of the following is an example activity employed by project teams to reduce waste and rework in an agile project? *Select the best answer.*

a. Leave the process unchanged, and remain steadfast to the plan
b. Deliver value infrequently, only at the major milestones or phase gates
c. Extend the feedback loops, to allow more stakeholders time to opine on product delivery
d. Reprioritize work, as needed, when changed requirements are identified

34.

Assigned as a project manager for Phase 2 of Skiddle M'Rink, Inc.'s CRM database update, Elysse notices the product features change regularly. Due to the modifications, the project team decides to adopt a

Flow-Based agile approach. Elysse should practice which activity to effectively manage the project? *Select the best answer.*

a. Regularly update the plans, to account for changing product feature delivery schedules
b. Extend the feedback loops, to allow more stakeholders time to opine on product delivery
c. Keep prioritization of requirements according to the original scope, as changes may result in scope creep
d. Preserve the process, as too much change may de-motivate the team

35.

Which one of the following is an example activity employed by project teams to reduce waste and rework in an agile project? *Select the best answer.*

a. Deliver value only at the major milestones, as phase-gates are the optimal time for stakeholders to evaluate product updates
b. Keep prioritization of requirements according to the original scope, as changes may result in scope creep
c. Frequent delivery of product, to enable early identification of issues and solutions
d. Extended feedback loops, allowing stakeholders time to review and evaluate product delivery

36.

Assigned as a project manager for Baker King, Inc., Taylor notices the development team continues to deliver product requiring significant rework each iterative cycle. What activity should Taylor recommend the project team follow to eliminate waste? *Select the best answer.*

a. Keep prioritization of requirements according to the original scope, as changes may result in scope creep
b. Incorporate short feedback loops, to gather stakeholder commentary on a more frequent basis
c. Deliver value only at the major milestones, as phase-gates are the optimal time for stakeholders to evaluate product updates
d. Extend the feedback loops, to allow more stakeholders time to opine on product delivery

37.

Which of the following is not regarded as an element of agile projects intended to reduce waste and rework? *Select the best answer.*

a. Extended feedback loops
b. Frequent adaptation of process
c. Regularly updated plans
d. Frequent delivery

38.

As the project manager for Big Box Retail, Inc., Caleb leads a cross-functional team to create a point of sale delivery system, using a new platform. Given the project characteristics, your team realizes the uncertainty is high across the project. What option should Caleb seek to stabilize the project? *Select the best answer.*

a. Request the developers take additional training courses on the new technology

b. Include more stakeholders on the team, so requirements can be added
c. Recommend more frequent Change Advisory Boards to address the uncertainty
d. Update the Risk Register to identify the risks and determine appropriate response plans

39.

According to Agile practice, which of the following statements is one of the twelve principles behind the Agile Manifesto? *Select the best answer.*

a. Business people and developers must work separately daily throughout the project.
b. Welcome changing requirements, even late in development. Agile processes harness change for the customer's competitive advantage.
c. Tollgate reviews are the primary measures of progress.
d. The best architectures, requirements, and designs emerge from large, structured teams.

40.

According to the Stacey Complexity Model, project teams may evaluate which two areas to determine project approach? *Select the best answer.*

a. Requirements, Technology
b. Requirements, Number of Stakeholders
c. Number of Stakeholders, Technology
d. Technology, Scope

41.

In the Predictive Project Life Cycle, activities are performed according to which cadence? *Select the best answer.*

a. Once for the entire project
b. Repeatedly, until correct
c. Once for a given increment
d. Multiple times, as defined by the Project Charter

42.

In the Iterative Project Life Cycle, activities are performed according to which cadence? *Select the best answer.*

a. Once for the entire project
b. Repeatedly, until correct
c. Once for a given increment
d. Multiple times, as defined by the Project Charter

43.

According to the Incremental Project Life Cycle practice, activities are performed according to which cadence? *Select the best answer.*

a. Once for the entire project
b. Repeatedly, until correct
c. Once for a given increment

d. Multiple times, as defined by the Project Charter

44.

The primary goal of the Predictive Project Life Cycle is to achieve which of the following objectives? *Select the best answer.*

a. Produce a solution with no rework
b. Deliver fast and often
c. Manage cost
d. Keep plan changes to a minimum

45.

According to the Incremental Project Life Cycle practice, product delivery is offered as per which of the following methods? *Select the best answer.*

a. Single delivery
b. At the end of each tollgate review
c. Frequent, small deliveries
d. At the end of the project

46.

A customer requires multiple updates and requirement changes based upon the most recent product review. What immediate action should the project manager take to ensure the project's goal is achieved according to the goal of the Agile Project Life Cycle? *Select the best answer.*

a. Propose frequent deliveries and obtain frequent customer feedback
b. Follow the Integrated Change Control process to escalate the revision request
c. Contact the project team to discuss the correct solution design
d. Do not proceed with the update, as the changes will alter the scheduled delivery commitment

47.

As a project manager, you confirm fixed Requirements under which project life cycle approach? *Select the best answer.*

a. Predictive life cycle
b. Iterative life cycle
c. Iterative life cycle
d. Incremental life cycle

48.

What should a project manager employing the Predictive Life Cycle project approach develop to aid in project success? *Select the best answer.*

a. A consistent, timeboxed approach, so the customer knows what to expect and when
b. A partial feature list for team and customer awareness
c. Detailed plans, so the team knows what to deliver and how
d. A workbreakdown charter, outlining the business case for the activities to be completed

49.

You work as a project manager for NewNorth Production, Inc., leading an agile team to implement a
new widget software platform. The development team will need to produce prototypes and proofs,
given some uncertainty around the technical needs. How should you proceed with the planning during
project execution? *Select the best answer.*

   a. Recommend creation of a separate team to manage the outputs as a separate project
   b. Keep the plans the same as defined at the beginning of the project, and handle outputs through
       Change Requests
   c. Recognize outputs from prototypes and proofs are expected, and the need to modify the plans
       created at the beginning of the project
   d. Document the outputs from the prototypes and proofs, and add the information as Lessons
       Learned for future projects

50.

Predictive projects require serialized sequence of work, as such business value is typically delivered at
the end of the project. *Select the best answer.*

   a. True
   b. False

51.

Under the Predictive Life Cycle approach, project team leaders aim to minimize _________. *Fill in the
blank.*

   a. Cost
   b. Team turnover
   c. Change
   d. Risks

52.

You recently assumed assignment as a project manager for an enterprise wide project. Due to the high
level of technical uncertainty, and multiple disagreements surrounding the requirements, you have
decided to employ a Predictive Life Cycle approach to managing the project. What phase should
commence the life cycle? *Select the best answer.*

   a. Design, as the project team needs to understand architectural logic and how the system will be
       developed
   b. Analyze, as the project team needs to understand what the customer wants via requirements
       gathering
   c. Build, as the project team starts building the design in iterative, incremental cycles
   d. Measure, to gather data to support the system design

53.

During a project team meeting, the project team members express frustration in the multiple delays
hindering the agile project. Due to frequent changes, influenced by disagreements amongst

stakeholders regarding views on the desired final product, tensions have started to run high within the team. You address the conflict directly, advising the team ____________________. *Select the best answer.*

    a. To take a deep breath, since the grumbling detracts from project objectives and delivery execution
    b. To stop complaining, as the team was aware of the potential for delays at the beginning of the project
    c. Iterative life cycles are not known for delays, and there is something wrong with the project
    d. Iterative life cycles may take longer because they are optimized for learning, rather than speed of delivery

54.

Which of the following statements best describes how Flow-based agile teams commence work on requested features? *Select the best answer.*

    a. The team waits for the customer to prioritize the work then works on all features simultaneously.
    b. The team pulls features from the backlog based on its capacity to work rather than on an iteration-based schedule.
    c. The team meets daily to discuss bandwidth, and pulls features from the backlog there is room for more work.
    d. The team sets the work plan at the beginning of the project, and works on features according to the scheduled defined at the beginning.

55.

What statement is typical for flow-based agile projects? *Select the best answer.*

    a. The team defines its workflow with columns on a task board and manages the work in progress for each column.
    b. The team sets the work plan at the beginning of the project, and works on features according to the scheduled defined at the beginning.
    c. The team ensures each feature takes the same amount of time to finish.
    d. The team keeps work-in-progress sizes large, to deliver as many features as possible to the customer.

56.

What statement is typical for iterative life cycle projects? *Select the best answer.*

    a. The team sets the work plan at the beginning of the project, and does not deviate from it.
    b. Each feature on the backlog may take a different amount of time to finish.
    c. The team defines its workflow with columns on a task board.
    d. Complexity is high, with requirements and features involving frequent changes

57.

You are running a major project for LassoTech, Inc., leading a cross-functional team to update the Compliance and Audit department's risk assessment application. Agile methodologies are new to the organization, as you were hired to aid the company in transitioning from traditional project management to the agile approach. There is some disagreement from stakeholders and the project team in how best to measure team progress. What advice do you share with the team in measuring progress for agile projects? *Select the best answer.*

a. Counsel the team that an incremental deliverable that is functional and provides value is the primary measure of progress for agile projects.
b. Instruct the team to work with stakeholders in creating a features backlog in partnership, since close collaboration in determining features is the primary measure of agile progress.
c. Guide the team in creating a detailed Gantt chart to display key milestones and deliverable dates as points for tracking success.
d. Inform the team customer satisfaction is the only measure of success.

58.

Agile life cycles combine both _________ and ________ approaches in order to adapt to high degrees of change and deliver project value more often. *Fill in the blank.*

a. Predictive, Agile
b. Iterative, Incremental
c. Traditional, Incremental
d. Predictive, Incremental

59.

What statement is true of agile projects? *Select the best answer.*

a. Customer satisfaction increases with early and continuous delivery of valuable products.
b. Customer satisfaction decreases as products are delivered incrementally, rather than all at one time.
c. Customer satisfaction is not important, as the primary goal of a project is to deliver on time and under budget.
d. Customer satisfaction increases, due to decreased time commitment since agile project teams are self-organizing.

60.

According to Agile practice, which of the following statements is one of the twelve principles behind the Agile Manifesto? *Select the best answer.*

a. Do not welcome changing requirements, even late in development.
b. Team collaboration is the primary measure of progress.
c. The project team works together frequently throughout the project.
d. Continuous attention to technical excellence and good design enhances agility.

61.

What is the primary benefit of employing the Incremental Project Life cycle framework? *Select the best answer.*

a. Project teams follow a deliberate plan, with activities and deliverables clearly defined for timely execution.

b. At the conclusion of each iteration, customers receive a subset of the core solution, allowing feedback to be incorporated in the upcoming iterative cycle.
c. Iterative cycles with short duration enable the team to better plan for upcoming release items and determine resource constraints.
d. Project managers can combine agile and predictive approaches, relying on flexibility and structure to drive product delivery.

62.

The Director of Engineering for your company recently contacted you. The agile project to which you have been assigned is challenged by requirements which seem to change daily. As the business customer identifies new modifications, your project team is beset by requests to provide prototypes for customer approval, in advance of actual product development. At project commencement, what is the best option the project team should have considered to address the modifications and prototype requests? **Select the best answer.**

a. Re-baselining the project at each phase gate review, to ensure the schedule and budget remain in alignment to project objectives.
b. Updating the Risk Register to catalogue new risks generating from lost productivity due to resources working on the prototypes rather than system requirements.
c. Ensuring an incremental life cycle approach would be followed, to address prototype and proof of concept requests for incorporation within upcoming iterative cycles.
d. Advising the business customer that modifications would only be considered upon adherence to the appropriate change control process.

63.

Your firm is considering a project which requires an initial investment of $500,000. The product from the project is forecasted to create revenues of $350,000 in the first year after the end of the project and of $125,000 in each of the two following years. What is true for the *net present value* of the project over the three year cycle at a *discount rate* of 10%?
Select the best answer.

a. $1,100,000
b. $100,000
c. $400,000
d. $15,401.95

64.

What does the term *proof of concept* refer to? **Select the best answer.**

a. A replication, on a much smaller scale, of a system or thing from which learning is desired
b. An early sample or model of product built to test a concept
c. Documented evidence, or a demonstration, that a requested design is feasible for application and solution to a business need.
d. A meeting facilitated by the Project Manager, and includes the Developers and Stakeholders to discuss system design concepts.

65.

Which of the following is generally not regarded as an aspect of a Minimum Viable Product (MVP)? ***Select the best answer.***

    a. Customer feedback to the team helps the team learn what details need to be added to the product for subsequent delivery.
    b. Customer value is delivered incrementally.
    c. Initial product development occurs based upon delivery of the complete set of features after gathering requirements from potential users.
    d. Minimum viable requirements are gathered during each iterative cycle, such that maximum product delivery can be achieved at the end of the project.

66.

You work as the senior project manager for the development of a new, high-tech sports complex. Due to design requirements around property features, the builder has elected to show you the finished office spaces of the new construction before continuing with the remainder of the arena complex. Therefore, you can see and approve style, fixtures, paint color, and flooring details, or request modifications, as necessary. Which of the following statements is not representative of the project life cycle approach utilized by the builder? ***Select the best answer.***

    a. Adjustments to time or money may need to be made, as customer-centric changes are potential factors for consideration.
    b. The builder has elected an approach which will reduce potential rework and hopefully end user dissatisfaction.
    c. The builder has elected an approach which will increase potential rework; however end user dissatisfaction should be minimized.
    d. The builder has elected an approach which will allow the project manager to see the value more often, relative to a predictive and deliberately planned project execution approach.

67.

What statement below is not a reason for employing an Iterative Life Cycle approach as a framework for managing a project? ***Select the best answer.***

    a. The business customer is unclear regarding product specifications, and the iterative approach will allow the project team time to progress towards a value-added solution.
    b. Customer feedback from viewing prototypes and proof of concepts can be incorporated more swiftly relative to traditional project management.
    c. The approach will foster trust and increased communication between the business customer and the project team.
    d. The project team can rely solely on prototypes and proof of concepts to deliver the product solution to the customer.

68.

How does an Agile project team best handle changing requirements and revised technical solutions prior to product delivery? ***Select the best answer.***

    a. Request detailed change requests and design documentation updates to ensure appropriate understanding regarding product requirements.

    b.   Have the project manager update the project charter and business case, to take into consideration the potential scope changes.

    c.   Ask the Stakeholders if the changing requirements are critical to product delivery, and if they are not, add the requirements to the backlog.

    d.   Consider the changing requirements, and evaluate how the modifications will impact existing design.

69.

What does *timebox* mean? ***Select the best answer.***

    a.   Any one of the common periods of time occurring during a 24 hour period (i.e., second, minute, hour, day)

    b.   A defined period of time during which a task must be completed.

    c.   An event marking a specific change or event in development.

    d.   A term used to identify the controlled progress from one phase to another phase.

70.

A combination of predictive, iterative, incremental, and/or agile approaches is a referred to as a _______ approach. ***Select the best answer.***

    a.   Combination

    b.   Planned Agile

    c.   Selective

    d.   Hybrid

71.

As a project manager recently assigned to a large-scale enterprise project, you realize the project would benefit for predictive planning at the beginning, but more agile practices in order to deliver the best value to the customer. The project Sponsor is a former project manager, and is a keen advocate of predictive planned projects. What should you propose to the project Sponsor regarding the project framework? ***Select the best answer.***

    a.   Advise the Sponsor it is not necessary to use a single approach for the entire project, and an agile approach would be critical for delivering continuous value to the customer.

    b.   Recommend the predictive planned approach, because that is the approach best understood by the Sponsor.

    c.   Request the project Sponsor obtain insight from senior leadership regarding the organization's strategy, and ensure the project framework aligns to the strategy.

    d.   Suggest a meeting with the project team, for clarity regarding their experience in agile practices.

72.

What is an example of a *Hybrid* Project Life Cycle approach? ***Select the best answer.***

    a.   A software project for AI applications in which high uncertainty, complexity and risk exists in the development portion at the beginning of the project, but is then followed by defined, repeatable rollout.

    b.   A software project for a high tech solution in which high uncertainty, complexity and risk have been deemed to exist throughout the life of the project.

c. A manufacturing project with definable certainty in development, complexity and risk throughout the life of product development.
d. A change management project with no development required, but training across 1,500+ sites and 8,000+ personnel is expected to be chaotic.

73.

Under the Hybrid Project Life Cycle approach __________ development is followed by _________ rollout. *Select the best answer.*

a. Planned, Predictive
b. Agile, Predictive
c. Iterative, Phased
d. Incremental, Phased

74.

Under the Combined Agile and Predictive Project Life Cycle Approach, the Agile Project Life Cycle and Predictive Project Life Cycle approaches are used _____________. *Select the best answer.*

a. Simultaneously
b. Sequentially
c. Independently
d. For 3 month incremental periods, then evaluated to determine product changes

75.

You recently assumed project management responsibilities for a software application project to test customer interest in gumball flavors. The project team is incrementally transitioning to agile, but still finds more comfort in delivering value via estimating time commitments in advance of performing activities, structuring work assignments according to specific time lines, and tracking progress for completion of interrelated tasks.

However, the business customer is keen to take receipt of incremental features of the applications, so that she can accurately determine the target pilot audience. What is an appropriate next step for you? *Select the best answer.*

a. Inform the business customer early receipt is not possible, as the team is more comfortable with adhering to the structured plan.
b. Recommend the project team decrease the iteration cycles for quicker delivery, and incorporate more agile practices such as Daily Standups and backlog grooming into standard project activities.
c. Review the project plan, and determine what tasks can be removed to speed up delivery of the product.
d. Update the Resource plan, as you will need to add team resources to meet the business customer's request.

76.

As a new project manager hired by FinRev Tech Solutions, Inc., you are assigned a project team managing the product delivery for a payment solution. The key stakeholder is the Director of Product Management-Payments, who is not pleased regarding the project's direction. Communication regarding product bugs identified in testing have contributed to release delays and complicated the relationship between the project team and the key stakeholder. Your first order of business is to transition the relationship back to more favorable terms. What activity can you do to meet this objective? ***Select the best answer.***

   a. Schedule Daily Standups with the Stakeholder and project team, to openly discuss project status and the main challenges hindering progress.
   b. Schedule a weekly meeting with just you and the Stakeholder, so that you can provide a status report regarding progress to date.
   c. Explain the team progress in the weekly project status report, and ensure the Stakeholder is included in the distribution.
   d. Do nothing, as the Stakeholder is a tyrant, as the project team has advised you that nothing you do will every please stakeholders.

77.
What is a *retrospective*? ***Select the best answer.***

   a. A document created at the conclusion of a project assessing team performance for project audit purposes.
   b. A justification regarding why the project did not achieve expected results.
   c. A meeting held at the conclusion of an iteration, to gather team feedback regarding positive actions which made the cycle productive, as well as changes the team should put into effect to make the next iteration more productive.
   d. A file containing the requirements and design documents, to be used as a future point of reference if questions arise regarding the closed project.

78.
The retrospective is most closely aligned to which traditional project management activity? ***Select the best answer.***

   a. Product showcase
   b. Milestone definition
   c. Quality checks
   d. Lessons Learned

79.
The figure below is an example of which project life cycle approach? ***Select the best answer.***

   a. Incremental life cycle approach
   b. Predominantly Predictive with some Agile approach
   c. Largely Agile with some Predictive approach
   d. Combined Agile and Predictive approach

80.
When is the retrospective performed? ***Select the best answer.***

a. At the close of the project
b. At the end of the iteration
c. At the end of the Monitoring & Control phase
d. During Daily Standup

Which of the following does not represent an example Hybrid Project Life Cycle approach? *Select the best answer.*

a. Agile development followed by a predictive rollout
b. Agile development and predictive approach employed simultaneously
c. Mostly predictive with some agile project components
d. Incremental development followed by agile project components

During planning discussions for the development of a multi-purpose arena complex, the team determines that while the majority of the property development requires routine, predictable work, some aspects of the development cycle will require more nimble practices. The project will entail using new to market siding materials for the first time, and the construction team needs time to experiment and adapt the materials before adding the final product to the facility space. What should the project manager propose as an optimal solution? *Select the best answer.*

a. Plan for a few small-scale installation trials first to determine the best installation method and to allow time for uncovering issues early in the process
b. Replace the new siding materials with a supply of traditional materials that the construction team has more familiarity
c. Add the siding materials to the facility space, and document the issues the construction team may experience during installation
d. Meet with the customer and the contractor representative and determine who is at fault for requesting a material which the construction team has not previously used

An approach which the project team addressed scope creep in an agile manner, with the remainder of the project managed predictively is representative of which Hybrid Project Life Cycle approach? *Select the best answer.*

a. Predictive Agile
b. Largely Predictive with Agile Components
c. Semi-Agile
d. Incremental Predictive

The Largely Agile approach with a Predictive Component is representative of which form of Project Life Cycle approach? *Select the best answer.*

a. Semi-Predictive

b. Hybrid
c. Predictive Agile
d. Incremental Agile

Which of the following statements is true regarding Agile frameworks? ***Select the best answer.***

a. Agile frameworks are customized for the team, due to the variety of approaches available.
b. Agile frameworks are not customized for the team, as the team may need to tailor practices to get results.
c. Once the team decides upon an Agile framework, it should not alter the framework practices throughout the life of the project.
d. Agile frameworks are not viable, workable solutions to manage projects successfully.

You are running a major data migration and system enhancement project, which includes three sub-projects. Although each of the sub-project managers manage their respective projects well, keeping tasks and deliverables on target according to scope objectives, the sub-project managers have voiced concern that they do not have enough insight to the core project. Specifically, the sub-project managers expressed lack of awareness in how their sub-projects benefit the organization as a whole.

You believe firmly that project managers should be servant leaders to the project team. How should you respond to the sub-project manager's concerns? ***Select the best answer.***

a. Work with the project team to clarify the 'why' or purpose, so they can engage around the common goal of the core project
b. Encourage the team to remain independent, as they have been successful to date in managing the sub-projects, and any change could disrupt the project execution
c. Tell the team it is best for the sub-projects to be optimized at the individual level, not the project level, as each project is unique
d. Review the output for each sub-project, and bring into your confidence only the project manager overseeing the best performing sub-project

Servant leadership refers to ____________? ***Select the best answer.***

a. Developing project team members to execute only to the tasks dictated by the project manager
b. Providing controlled direction to the project team, without obtaining meaningful participation from the project team
c. Enlightening the project team regarding customer requirements, and ensuring the team serves the customer's needs
d. Leading through service to the team, focusing on understanding and addressing the needs and development of team members

Which of the statements is not true regarding project manager's functioning as servant leaders of the project? ***Select the best answer.***

a. Once the purpose is established, the project manager should encourage the team to create an environment where everyone can succeed.
b. Project managers should ask team member to contribute only to their assigned deliverable.
c. In evaluating the project status, the project manager should look to the project results, rather than attempting to follow the "perfect" agile process.
d. The entire team optimizes the project level, not the person level

89.

You recently assigned project team members to activities, and desire to direct the project through the demonstration of servant leadership qualities. Which of the following behaviors should you exemplify to the team? *Select the best answer.*

a. Controlling behavior vs coaching behavior
b. Snooping
c. Listening
d. Neglecting

90.

The project team members have been assigned 60% to your project, and in general meet customer demand sporadically. In a recent meeting with the project Sponsor, the Sponsor reported some business customers have not been pleased with the irregular delivery pattern. The most recent status report reflected slight delays for key deliverables expected over the next quarter. You notified the Sponsor that team members have been spending less than 60% of their time working on your project, due to project conflicts.

The Sponsor offered support, and authorized 100% allocation of team members. What can you now propose to the team to address project delivery going forward? *Select the best answer.*

a. Suggest the team adopts a flow-based cadence, allowing for regular, defined timeboxes to support quicker value delivery to business customers
b. Recommend the team exceed WIP limits to get back on schedule for quarterly delivery
c. Urge the team to work extra hours to make up for the lost time and productivity associated with the erratic delivery
d. Consider training the team on scaled agile, to scale the project across various teams as a means to speed up execution

91.

Project team members have been assigned 100% to your project, however, in general the quality of the product increments has been poor. In a recent meeting with the project Sponsor, the Sponsor reported some business customers have been displeased with the product, receiving little value in the deliveries. What can you propose to the team to improve product quality and value? *Select the best answer*.

a. The team should think about what they consider to be the most valuable features, and develop the attributes accordingly.
b. The team should schedule time with business customers subsequent to each delivery cycle, to document feedback and add the items to the Parking Lot.

    c.   The team should consider using a test-driven development practice to aid in identifying defects early and developing mitigating solutions before product delivery.

    d.   The team should continue according to the current process, and quality and value are subjective product attributes, anyway.

92.

Project team members have been assigned 100% to your project, however, the flow of work has been interrupted by various delays and impediments. You recently met with the project Sponsor, who reported business customers have been displeased with the product, due to the intermittent delivery and delays. What can you propose to the team to improve product delivery going forward? ***Select the best answer***.

    a.   The team should evaluate WIP limits and exceed target levels, as the delivery flow will work out in the end.

    b.   The team should work extra hours to make up for the delays.

    c.   The team should create a sub-QA process responsible for identifying defects and recommending appropriate solutions to the business customer.

    d.   The team should consider using Kanban boards to make work visible and experimenting with WIP limits to improve flow.

93.

Project team members have been assigned 100% to your project, however, the delivery of product features is still insufficient relative to customer demand. In a recent meeting with the business customers and project Sponsor, some customers expressed frustration and annoyance regarding the fact that product features remain absent or deficient, despite multiple promises for delivery. During the review for features completed per the previous iteration, many customers noted the incomplete product elements. You advise the Sponsor the agile project team is already working at full capacity, and adding to the team's workload will be a significant de-motivator.

What recommendation can you propose to the Sponsor to improve product delivery going forward? ***Select the best answer***.

    a.   Suggest scaling the feature development across one or several agile teams, as long as the ability to scale can be accomplished with minimal disruption

    b.   Advocate for a better incentive structure for the team, with the incentive payouts made to the team in association with the team achieving target delivery dates

    c.   Request more resources be added to the team, because if you are able to double team size you will be able to deliver the features to meet customer demand.

    d.   Veto any work associated with incomplete features, and require the business customer to accept the product as-is

94.

Your Director of Technology has been impressed with your project management and performance skills over the past year, as you successfully executed three key initiatives in meeting customer, stakeholder, and organizational objectives. You have been recommended for another high-profile assignment, one which entails the transition from waterfall and implementation of an agile framework to better achieve operating strategy. Project team members are inexperienced in the use of agile approaches. In this situation, you should consider what action? ***Select the best answer.***

a. Mandate that all team members become certified in at least 1 agile methodology before implementing an agile approach
b. Test the project team members on their agile knowledge, and if they demonstrate minimum proficiency, proceed full steam ahead with the transition!
c. Effect an immediate transition from waterfall to agile, as you believe the team can learn key concepts quickly on their own without additional training downtime
d. Start by training the team members in the fundamentals of the agile mindset and principles, providing workshops or Lunch 'N Learns on the approaches so the team can learn how best to adopt and use the methodology

95.

Following your recent assignment to lead an agile project team to deliver new mobile application solution for the enterprise, you review the firm's organizational structure to assess potential team depth. The Technology Manager has given you approval to contact and onboard the necessary personnel you deem important for project execution. Your next step is to request a roadmap meeting to brainstorm ideas. What exactly should that team look like? *Select the best answer.*

a. A cross-functional team comprised of the organizational department leads, as they would best understand how to align customer requirements and organizational goals
b. A functional team of developers only, as they have the best experience in developing the code necessary for the mobile application
c. A cross-functional team comprised of designers, developers, testers, and any other required roles to best deliver finished work in the shortest possible time, with higher quality
d. A functional team with deep Marketing digital content expertise, as the mobile application is targeted towards external customers

96.

Which of the following statements is a typical description for the role the Product Owner performs in the agile team? *Select the best answer.*

a. The Product Owner facilitates the team meetings, guiding the direction of team interactions.
b. The Product Owner is the servant leader, coaching the team regarding product features needed to satisfy customer requirements.
c. The Product Owner designs the product, as he or she often has domain expertise in system schemes and architecture.
d. The Product Owner work with teams daily, providing product feedback and setting direction on the next piece of functionality to be developed/delivered.

97.

Which of the following statements is a typical description of the skills required for the Team facilitator role in the agile team? *Select the best answer.*

a. Servant Leadership skills of facilitation, coaching, and impediment removal
b. Directive Leadership skills of decision-making, administration, and task definition
c. Authoritarian Leadership skills of precise goal planning, controlled discussions, unilateral organization
d. Transformational Leadership skills of inspiration, follow through, and motivation

Which position below is not considered to be a role typically found in an Agile team? *Select the best answer.*

a. The individual who works with stakeholders, customers, and the team to define the product direction.
b. The neutral party assigned to help the team understand, and achieve, its common objective.
c. The recipient of the product or features delivered via the project team.
d. An employee from any level of the organization who represents domain expertise of a specific functional area.

As the project manager assigned to a high performance agile project team, you have requested the team focus on a specific feature to meet delivery objectives. You notice that one developer can test some areas of the product and develop different areas of the product. Which of the following attributes describes the type of person who is a generalized specialist? *Select the best answer.*

a. ZigZag person
b. T-shaped person
c. I-shaped person
d. Talented specialist

Retrospectives best reflect which of the 12 principles outline in the Agile Manifesto? *Select the best answer.*

a. Continuous attention to technical excellence and good design enhances agility.
b. At regular intervals, the team reflects on how to become more effective, then tunes and adjusts its behavior accordingly.
c. Agile processes promote sustainable development. The sponsors, developers, and users should be able to maintain a constant pace indefinitely.
d. Build projects around motivated individuals. Give them the environment and support they need, and trust them to get the job done

Your firm is considering a project which requires an initial investment of $500,000. The product from the project is forecasted to create revenues of $350,000 in the first year after the end of the project and of $125,000 in each of the two following years. What is true for the *present value* of the expected cash flows over the three year cycle at a *discount rate* of 10%? *Select the best answer.*

a. $1,100,000
b. $600,000
c. $515,401.95
d. $495,200.15

While executing a project, you sense a slightly downbeat attitude in your dispersed team. Communication is poor and knowledge sharing has been inadequate to support positive team dynamics. You decide to establish a video conferencing link between the various locations, to encourage free exchange of ideas and spontaneous engagement amongst team members. Which type of communication portal did you establish? *Select the best answer.*

   a. Daily Standup
   b. Remote Pairing
   c. Fishbowl Window
   d. Retrospective

103.

You are leading a dispersed agile team in charge of developing a digital content platform for your organization. The project is a high priority focus for senior leadership, hence the most knowledgeable resources have been picked across On Shore and Off Shore resources. You notice knowledge dependencies between the dispersed team of developers, and any delay in transitioning feature development work could significantly impact delivery objectives. You decide to establish a video conference so that the developers can share screens and connect as needed for face-to-face pairing. Which type of communication standard did you establish? *Select the best answer.*

   a. eXtreme Programming
   b. Remote Pairing
   c. Fishbowl Window
   d. Technical Driven Design

104.

As a project manager, you note that your organization is beset by silos across the business functions. In order to promote better engagement and value delivery, you should recommend what action to functional managers? *Select the best answer.*

   a. Managers should focus on flow efficiency rather than resource efficiency to drive value delivery.
   b. Managers should focus on resource efficiency rather than flow efficiency to drive value delivery.
   c. Managers should focus on completing tasks within the committed terms of the project schedule to drive value delivery.
   d. Managers should focus on training resources for clarity of performance goals to drive value delivery.

105.

Which technique can an agile project manager employ to promote the successful adoption of an agile mindset when forming an agile team? *Select the best answer.*

   a. Share the detailed project plan so the team is aware of the target activities, and encourage the team to share feedback and concerns
   b. Schedule a kick-off meeting to include only the project team members and clearly communicate the project goals and objectives
   c. Let the team self-organize regarding the agile framework they feel most knowledgeable about and adopt the practices, accordingly
   d. Build a foundation of trust and safety amongst team members

As a project manager, you believe a team charter should be developed for the project team. What is the team charter? *Select the best answer.*

a. The document describes how the team will communicate with business customers and key stakeholders.
b. The document defines team norms, to ensure full understanding of how the project team should best engage with one another.
c. The document defines the project purpose, main stakeholders, and key roles and responsibilities.
d. The document contains all the feature requirements to be developed by the team.

What is another name for the team's social contract? *Select the best answer*

a. Project Plan
b. Communication Plan
c. Project Charter
d. Team Charter

What is the purpose of the project vision? *Select the best answer.*

a. Articulate the goals of the project
b. Communicate who will benefit from the project's accomplishment
c. Define the release criteria
d. Create an environment for team member engagement

During execution in an agile project to build a new customer web portal, you experience the loss of a team member to another high priority project. A new resource has been assigned as a replacement. What can you share with the resource to clarify the upcoming features to be built to avoid technical delays in delivery? *Select the best answer.*

a. Give the resource the detailed System Design Document which details system requirements, per product feature requests
b. Provide the feedback from the Retrospectives, in which the team noted some of the feature gaps which need to be considered in future releases
c. Share the Product Backlog, which contains the ordered list of all the work identified by the Product Owner, as features to be developed
d. Offer the resource the Business Requirements Document which chronicles the customer's product specifications

Which of the following items is used to show the anticipated sequence of features to be delivered? *Select the best answer.*

a. Business Requirements Document
b. Project Plan
c. Product Roadmap
d. Project Charter

For the Flow-Based Project Life Cycle approach, which technique is optimally suited for backlog refinement? *Select the best answer.*

a. Predictive Iteration Backlog refinement
b. Precise Iteration Backlog refinement
c. Just-in-time Backlog refinement
d. Daily discussions around stories coming up for development

The *impact map* is used to support which goal? *Select the best answer.*

a. Aid teams in aligning their activities with overall business objectives and make better decisions
b. Report the current situation with regard to a business, project, or subject matter
c. Describe the product features requested by the business customer
d. Compare actual performance relative to potential, or desired, performance

During backlog refinement, you notice the Product Owner is not quite certain about a few interrelated features requested by business customers. The lack of feature clarity proposes much risk to the project. Which should you do as the project manager to deal with the uncertainty? *Select the best answer.*

a. Offer to add the issue around feature uncertainty to the Parking Lot for future discussion
b. Recommend the team spike the story to understand the technical and business risks
c. Add the feature items to the Risk Register and proceed with development since the risks have been noted
d. Include the features in the upcoming iteration and document findings for review with the Product Owner

Which question is not typically asked, or answered, by agile team members during Daily Standup? *Select the best answer.*

a. What do we need to do to advance this piece of work?
b. What do we need to finish as a team?
c. Are there any bottlenecks or blockers to the flow of work?
d. What do we need to do to make the next iteration more successful?

During the Daily Standup, you notice a pattern has occurred over the past few meetings. The meeting has become a means for the team to begin solving identified problems, as key resources are available and the Product Owner's schedule has little flexibility in arranging additional discussions. The project manager should advocate which of the following actions? *Select the best answer.*

a. Continue to use the Daily Standup for problem solving, since the problem is realized during the meeting, and the Product Owner does not have availability to meet at any other time
b. Add the identified issues to a parking lot, and create a separate meeting to discuss the items of concern
c. Advise the team not to escalate critical issues during the meeting, as it has become too distracting meeting.
d. Abbreviate the Daily Standup to 5 minutes, and work with the team to only discuss the critical problems during the remaining 10 minutes

116.

Being the project manager for an agile project team, the project life cycle your team has employed to execute the project is iteration-based agile. When is completed work demonstrated to the business customer? *Select the best answer.*

a. Beginning of the next iteration
b. End of the current iteration
c. End of the project
d. During the iteration

117.

What is typical for demonstrating product features developed under the Flow-Based agile framework? *Select the best answer.*

a. Product features are shown at the conclusion of the project.
b. The project team performs a product review at the end of the iteration.
c. Product features are shown whenever the Product Owner demands to view the completed features.
d. Product features are demonstrated when enough work has been completed to deliver a comprehensible solution.

118.

During a meeting with the project team, you discuss the critical aspect of delivering value to the customer. One technique the team recently employed concerns the recurrent incorporation of developed features into the product, with retesting performed to validate product performance? What agile practice is the team utilizing? *Select the best answer.*

a. User Acceptance Testing
b. Continuous integration
c. Value delivery
d. Gap analysis

119.

Prior to deploying the product features into production, the team coordinates testing to validate features meet business customer needs. What testing technique evaluates the complete and integrated software solution relative to system compliance with specified requirements? *Select the best answer.*

a. Unit testing

b.   Acceptance testing
c.   Smoke testing
d.   Integration testing

120.

In Acceptance Test-Driven Development, what is the appropriate order of activities? *Select the best answer.*

a.   The team discusses the product Acceptance Criteria, creates the tests, then writes the code and automated tests to validate the Acceptance Criteria.
b.   The team discusses the product Acceptance Criteria, writes the code, then creates the automated tests which validate the Acceptance Criteria.
c.   The team creates the tests to validate the Acceptance Criteria, writes the code, then creates the automated tests to validate the Acceptance Criteria.
d.   The team validates the Acceptance Criteria, creates the tests, writes the code, then creates automated tests to validate the Acceptance Criteria.

121.

You recently have been assigned new testers to test the code developed for a digital content software product solution. The testers are used to testing under the ATDD framework, but your project entails TDD testing. What should you advise your new testers regarding TDD testing? *Select the best answer.*

a.   Automated tests should be written before creating the product.
b.   TDD is not an effective way to mistake-proof the product, and glean more insight regarding their experience with ATDD.
c.   Automated tests should be written after creating the product.
d.   Automated tests are not useful, and the testers will need to create detailed test scripts to be executed manually.

122.

What is the meaning of the term *spike*? *Select the best answer.*

a.   A story which may entail additional cost and rework due to the implementation of an easy solution now.
b.   A story that is placed on the Product Backlog until the project team is ready to commit to development.
c.   A story that cannot be estimated until a development team runs a timeboxed investigation.
d.   A story to simplify the design of existing code.

123.

Your organization is in the process of transitioning from waterfall to agile practices, and as such some agile routines are still relatively new to PMO personnel. Your project team is near completion of its third iteration, and in 2 days the team will demonstrate product features completed during the most recent iterative cycle. What action can you take to educate the organization on agile best practices and routines? *Select the best answer.*

a. Invite the PMO Director to the demonstration, and request other PMO personnel not attend as the agile project team is still learning best practices.
b. Invite the PMO and other interested personnel to the demonstration so they can see project progress.
c. Exclude the PMO and other personnel from the demonstration as it may make the project team nervous in their presentation delivery.
d. Record the demonstration and place the video on the organization's intranet site so the entire organization see the best practice directly.

124.

If the agile project team is unclear regarding its purpose or mission, what should the project manager do to re-direct the team? *Select the best answer.*

a. Distribute the Project Plan and request feedback if the team does not understand the deliverables and timelines.
b. Review the Agile charter with the team to reiterate vision, mission, and mission tests.
c. Discuss the Business Requirements documents to ensure the project team understands the features to be developed.
d. Evaluate the product backlog and remove any product features which are contributing to team confusion.

125.

In an agile project environment, which of the following statements is true? *Select the best answer.*

a. Agile teams see and fix problems less frequently than predictive teams.
b. Surrogate measurements, such as percent done, are more useful than empirical measurements, such as finished features.
c. Empirical measurements, such as finished features, are more useful than surrogate measurements, such as percent done.
d. Agile teams identify problems more frequently than predictive teams, but wait until the end of the project to fix the problems during the final iteration.

126.   41

Your project work is nearly finished, and the project Sponsor has requested you put together a list of qualitative and quantitative measures to review team performance. What is not an example of a qualitative measure? *Select the best answer.*

a. Team morale
b. Business satisfaction with delivered features
c. Continuous improvement
d. Team velocity

127.

As your project draws to a close, you want to be proactive in listing a few quantitative measures for team performance. What is not an example of a quantitative measure? *Select the best answer.*

a. Throughput
b. Features completed

c. Continuous improvement
d. Team velocity

128.

With its focus measuring what the team delivers, not what the team predicts it will deliver, agile practices tend to favor ______________ measurements? *Select the best answer.*

a. Value-based
b. Hypothetical
c. Speculative
d. Predictive

129.

You are running an enterprise project with a purpose of transitioning the organization to a paperless environment. The project Sponsor has tasked you with determining how long it will take to complete the remaining stories in the backlog. If there are 40 stories remaining on the backlog, and the team averages a cycle time of 2 days per story, what estimate can you share with the project Sponsor regarding the number of days remaining until development completion? *Select the best answer.*

a. 100 days
b. 80 days
c. 40 days
d. 20 days

130.

You are running an enterprise project to deliver a new ERP platform for the Accounting department. You have been tasked with determining how long it will take to complete the remaining stories in the backlog. If the team averages 75 story points per iteration, and rough estimates indicate there are 675 points remaining, what estimate can you share with the project Sponsor regarding the number of iterative cycles remaining until development completion? *Note: Assume no additional product refinement is required. Select the best answer.*

a. 75 iterations
b. 50 iterations
c. 15 iterations
d. 9 iterations

131.

If your project team averages 65 story points per 2-week iteration, and rough estimates indicate there are 725 points remaining for feature development, what estimate can you share with the project Sponsor regarding the approximate timeframe for development completion? *Note: Assume no additional product refinement is required. Select the best answer.*

a. 5.5 months
b. 4.5 months
c. 3.5 months
d. 2.5 months

You work as a project manager for Doleo, Inc., and are leading a cross-functional team to update the Sales department's reporting application. There is uncertainty regarding the application development, but the team has decided to progress towards execution, with oversight by the Product Owner. What is the best manner to manage the feature uncertainty? *Select the best answer.*

a. Request the Product Owner clarify all outstanding questions regarding feature needs prior to adding the feature to the backlog.
b. Evaluate the backlog, tag all stories that have elements of uncertainty, and move them to the bottom of the request list.
c. Re-design the features to remove ambiguity, as per the team's assessment.
d. Review the empirical data from features completed in prior iterations, and re-plan small increments based upon learnings gleaned.

The _________________ depicts the remaining story points plotted relative to time remaining in the iteration. *Select the best answer.*

a. Story point chart
b. Gantt chart
c. Burndown chart
d. Burnup chart

In reviewing the teams progress, the project manager notices by Day 7 of the 10-day iteration, the bottom line on the Burndown chart indicates 15 story points and the top line on the chart indicates 25 points. What can the project manager infer from her review of the Burndown chart? *Select the best answer.*

a. The team is behind schedule.
b. The Burndown chart does not reflect the team's commitment to execution.
c. The team is on schedule to complete the features by the end of the iteration.
d. The team is ahead of ahead of initial estimations.

The _________________ depicts the story points completed relative to time remaining in the iteration. *Select the best answer.*

a. Story point chart
b. Burnup chart
c. Burndown chart
d. Gantt chart

According to the Burnup chart below, the team completed approximately how many story points between 2/01/2013 and 6/01/2013? *Select the best answer.*

a. 0 points

b.   5 points
c.   7 points
d.   10 points

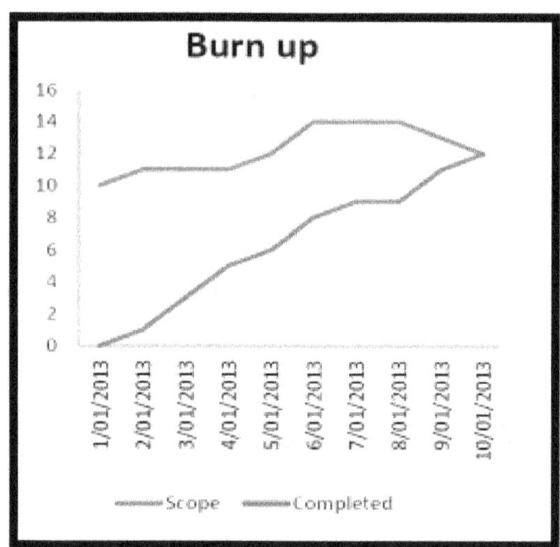

137.

According to the chart below, by 8/01/2013, the project team had completed __________. *Select the best answer.*

a.   … more story points than estimated to be completed by 8/01/2013
b.   … less story points than estimated to be completed by 8/01/2013
c.   … the same story points as estimated to be completed by 8/01/2013
d.   … no story points by 8/01/2013

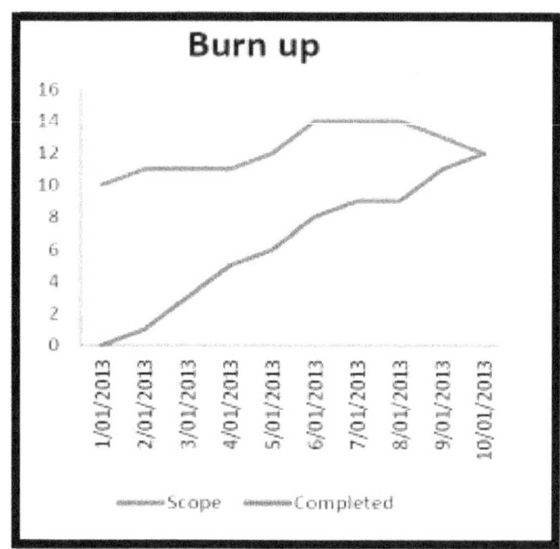

138.

In calculating the team velocity at the end of the iteration, you notice the number of story points completed is once again lower than velocity points associated with other project teams. Your project Sponsor asked about the discrepancy, and thinks your project team's performance is insufficient relative to your colleagues. What should you advise the Sponsor? ***Select the best answer.***

   a.   Comparing velocities across teams should be avoided, as velocity is a function of a variety of factors which will differ across teams.
   b.   Addressing the performance with the team is your highest priority, and the issue will be discussed during the next Retrospective.
   c.   Other project teams have higher performing resources, and you have requested a team resource shift for the next iteration.
   d.   Velocity is not an accurate measure of team performance.

139.

Capacity measures the amount of work the project team is capable of achieving in the upcoming iteration, while ____________ measures the amount of work completed during the iteration.

   a.   Throughput
   b.   Velocity
   c.   Yield
   d.   Burnup

140.

Which measurement is commonly used by project teams to determine bottlenecks and delays which may hinder project execution? ***Select the best answer.***

   a.   Yield
   b.   Velocity
   c.   Throughput
   d.   Cycle time

141.

Cycle time is defined as ….. ***Select the best answer.***

   a.   … the time you start the task until the time the feature is placed into production.
   b.   … the time the feature is placed on the backlog until the time it is removed from production.
   c.   … the time you start until the time you complete the task.
   d.   … the time you start the task until the time the Product Owner accepts the feature.

142.

Lead time is defined as _______________. ***Select the best answer.***

   a.   … the time between story placement on the backlog until system decommission.
   b.   … the time between story placement on the backlog until the feature is removed from production.
   c.   … the time between commencement of development until development completion.
   d.   … the time between story placement on the board until story delivery to the customer.

143.

Prior to iteration planning, you become aware that 2 team members will be out of the office a few days during the upcoming iteration. You need to provide your project Sponsor with a preliminary estimate regarding team capacity over the next few weeks. What items can you review to attain an initial assessment for measuring team capacity given the resource constraints? *Select the best answer.*

    a.   Burnup and Burndown charts from previous iterations
    b.   Team charter
    c.   Cycle times
    d.   Iteration backlog

144.

Reaction time is defined as ______________. *Select the best answer.*

    a.   ... the time between Ready and placement of the story in the first column on the board, as a measure to determine the response time for new requests.
    b.   ... the time between Ready and start of development.
    c.   ... the time between Ready and Done.
    d.   ... the time between Ready and placement of the feature in production.

145.

As the project manager for a digital transformation project, you track the SPI (schedule performance index) to monitor how well your agile project is performing relative to schedule goals.   If the team has capacity to complete 50 story points during an iteration, and completed 45 story points, then what do you inform your project Sponsor regarding team performance? *Select the best answer.*

    a.   The team is working at 111% of the target rate planned.
    b.   The team is working at 100% of the target rate planned.
    c.   The team is working at 90% of the target rate planned.
    d.   The team is working at 80% of the target rate planned.

146.

As the project manager for a program strategy project, you track the SPI (schedule performance index) to monitor how well your agile project is performing relative to schedule goals.   If the team has capacity to complete 35 story points during an iteration, and completed 45 story points, what is the SPI? *Select the best answer.*

    a.   1.28
    b.   1.00
    c.   0.77
    d.   0.45

147.

As the project manager for a CRM implementation project, you track the CPI (cost performance index) to monitor how well your agile project is performing relative to cost targets.   If the value of completed features to date is $1.5 million relative to actual costs to date of $1.8 million, then what do you inform your project Sponsor regarding earned value to date? *Select the best answer.*

a.   The project value reflects earned value of $1.20 on the dollar compared to plan.
b.   The project value reflects earned value of $1.00 on the dollar compared to plan.
c.   The project value reflects earned value of $0.83 on the dollar compared to plan.
d.   The project value reflects earned value of $0.80 on the dollar compared to plan.

148.

As the project manager for a digital transformation project, you track the CPI (cost performance index) to monitor how well your agile project is performing relative to cost objectives.   If the team has incurred costs to date of $2.0 million relative to completed features value of $2.4 million, then what is the SPI? *Select the best answer.*

a. $1.50
b. $1.20
c. $0.83
d. $0.75

149.

One key service a traditional PMO may provide in its transformation to a more robust, agile center of excellence is ___________? *Select the best answer.*

a.   Perform tollgate reviews
b.   Audit project plans, milestones, and all project artifacts
c.   Facilitate organizational learning
d.   Develop the RACI matrix

150.

What statement below reflects a service high performing agile centers of excellence can perform to effectively manage stakeholders? *Select the best answer.*

a.   Tutor subject matter experts
b.   Offer unit testing instruction
c.   Provide product owner training
d.   Prepare retrospective findings

151.

Which statement is not reflective of an institutional roadblock to organizational agility? *Select the best answer.*

a.   Leaders are rewarded for local inefficiencies rather than end-to-end flow delivery.
b.   Procurement is based upon short-term pricing strategies.
c.   Employees are I-shaped specialists with few tools or no motivation to diversity skillset
d.   Department engagement is highly collaborative, with an organizational mindset of delivering early and often.

152.

As the core identity of the enterprise, _________________ is represented by the attitudes, values, believes, and behaviors exhibited by the firm's employees. *Select the best answer.*

a. The enterprise environmental factor
b. An organizational process asset
c. Organizational culture
d. The stakeholder

153.

Which statement below is representative of an organization embracing project management within its cultural framework? *Select the best answer.*

a. Supporting projects in isolation from organizational strategy
b. Engaging project sponsors at the executive level
c. Segmenting projects from organizational vision, mission statement, and objectives
d. Maintaining an unstructured approach to project management

154.

Which of the following statements is not a recognized attribute of collocated agile teams? *Select the best answer.*

a. Better communication
b. Knowledge sharing
c. Reduced cost of learning
d. Develop and deliver often

155.

Which of the following statements is not a recognized attribute of agile teams? *Select the best answer.*

a. Inter-team dependency to deliver
b. Encouraging disparate approaches to work
c. Simplifying team cost
d. Preserving intellectual capital

156.

One method project managers can utilize to allay the pain point of __________ is to progressively decompose roadmap into backlog of smaller, concrete requirements. *Select the best answer.*

a. Unclear requirements
b. Poor user experience
c. Defects
d. Team conflict

157.

One method project managers can utilize to allay the pain point of __________ is to split stories or use agile modeling and spikes to understand story context. *Select the best answer.*

a. Customer feedback
b. Inaccurate estimation
c. Unclear work assignments

d. Degraded code quality

158.

In agile, the _________________ is used to drives the quality of work and is used to assess when a user story is complete. ***Select the best answer.***

  a. Business requirement
  b. Velocity
  c. Feature development
  d. Definition of done

159.

You work as a project manager for GoGoGo.com, Inc., leading the design and implementation of a software application. Due to internal resource knowledge gaps, a portion of the project will require outsourcing development to a third party vendor. You schedule a meeting with the Director of Procurement to review contract options and ensure the correct timelines are outlined within the sourcing agreement.

Both the organization and outsourcing firm agreed upon a fixed budget, however, the supplier offered your firm the opportunity to vary the project scope to ensure capacity fit and incorporation of potential innovation opportunities. This contract is representative of what contract form? ***Select the best answer.***

  a. Dynamic scope option
  b. Fixed price
  c. Not to exceed time and materials
  d. Graduated time and materials

160.

A collaborative approach to contracting, _______________ embeds the supplier's skilled workers directly into the customer's organization. This tactic represents what contract form? ***Select the best answer.***

  a. Partnership management
  b. Team augmentation
  c. Graduated time and materials
  d. Fixed price

161.

An example characteristic demonstrating an organization's readiness for change is _____________. ***Select the best answer.***

  a. Executive management's willingness to change
  b. Organization's willingness to maintain its views, outlooks, and culture
  c. Focus on long-term goals versus short-term budgeting and metrics
  d. Talent management inexperience

162.

Which of the following EEFs is internal to the organization? ***Select the best answer.***

a. Geographic distribution of facilities and resources
b. Legal restrictions
c. Commercial databases
d. Academic research

Which statement is not accurate regarding the project manager's role in the project? *Select the best answer.*

a. Project managers are expected to perform every role in the project, as their knowledge and skills provide critical direction for the team.
b. Project managers area not expected to perform every role on the project, but should possess project management knowledge and experience to direct the team.
c. Project managers should communicate promptly to the team, via written communications or face to face meetings, as appropriate.
d. Project managers should demonstrate technical, leadership, strategic, and business management skills to provide critical direction for the team.

Project managers use___________ to alleviate conflict and balance competing goals presented by project stakeholders. *Select the best answer.*

a. Control
b. Technical skills
c. Interpersonal skills
d. Intimidation

The ideal Talent Triangle skills demonstrated by a project manager include _____________. *Select the best answer.*

a. Technical, Leadership and Regulator
b. Leadership, Strategic and business management, and Technical
c. Strategic and business management, Regulator, Technical
d. Regulator, Interpersonal, Business Management

Which of the following is not a process within Project Integration Management? *Select the best answer.*

a. Develop Project Charter
b. Manage Project Knowledge
c. Monitor and Control Project Work
d. Collect Requirements

___________________ is the project Knowledge Area that is specific to project managers, such that accountability for executing this component cannot be transferred to another team member. *Select the best answer.*

a. Project Cost Management
b. Project Risk Management
c. Project Integration Management
d. Project Schedule Management

Project managers may need to adapt or modify the Project Integration Management processes to affect a successful project execution. Which question is not a consideration the project manager should contemplate? *Select the best answer.*

a. What is an appropriate project life cycle for project execution?
b. What development life cycle and approach are appropriate for the product, service, or result?
c. How many times can the team extend the project schedule beyond the original finish date before value is lost to the stakeholders?
d. How will knowledge be managed in the project to foster a collaborative working environment?

Considerations for tailoring Project Integration Management processes include the following, except __________. *Select the best answer.*

a. Management approaches
b. Knowledge management
c. Project life cycle
d. Contract management

In an agile/adaptive project environment, control of the detailed product planning and delivery is the responsibility of the __________. *Select the best answer.*

a. Team
b. Project manager
c. Business stakeholders
d. Business customer

Which of the following is not a process within Project Scope Management? *Select the best answer.*

a. Create WBS
b. Validate Scope
c. Collect Requirements
d. Control Quality

You work as a project manager for Chi Me, LLC and are leading a cross-functional team to update the Sales department's reporting applications. You have scheduled a meeting with the Sales Director to review the required work necessary to deliver the product, according to the specified features and functions. What is the context of the meeting? *Select the best answer.*

a. To discuss product scope
b. To discuss project scope
c. To review service deadlines
d. To baseline the project

173.

Which two processes are repeated during each iteration occurring within an adaptive life cycle? *Select the best answer.*

a. Validate Schedule, Control Schedule
b. Validate Cost, Control Cost
c. Validate Scope, Control Scope
d. Validate Risk, Control Risk

174.

An output of Validate scope is _______________. *Select the best answer.*

a. Revised Gantt chart
b. Accepted deliverables
c. Updated risk register
d. Supplier contract

175.

Projects which involve evolving requirements, in which scope is defined and refined throughout the project are known as _____________. *Select the best answer.*

a. Infrastructure projects
b. Chaotic projects
c. Predictive projects
d. Agile projects

176.

Which item below is not an Organizational Process Asset that can influence Plan Scope Management processes? *Select the best answer.*

a. Policies
b. Procedures
c. Historical Information
d. Phase closure documents

177.

Which item is not a component of the scope management plan? *Select the best answer.*

a. Preparing a project scope statement
b. Establishing how the scope baseline will be approved and maintained
c. Enabling the creation of the schedule baseline from the detailed project scope statement
d. Specifying how formal acceptance of the completed project deliverables will be obtained

178.

The _____________________ is a component of the project management plan that describes how the scope will be defined, developed, monitored, controlled, and validated. ***Select the best answer.***

   a. Contract provision
   b. Cost management plan
   c. Quality management plan
   d. Scope management plan

179.

In leading a cross-functional team, you manage a project to implement a new resource management application for your organization. The project is in the initial stages; thus, you are still in the process of establishing discussions around product needs. You gather a group of stakeholders together to meet in an effort to generate and collect multiple ideas related to project and product requirements. This method is what form of data gathering technique? ***Select the best answer.***

   a. Brainstorming
   b. Expert judgement
   c. Delphi method
   d. Interviews

180.

_______________ involves comparing products or processes to those of comparable organizations to identify best practices. ***Select the best answer.***

   a. Feature development
   b. Backlog refinement
   c. Cost benefit analysis
   d. Benchmarking

181.

Which of the following is not a process within Project Schedule Management? ***Select the best answer.***

   a. Determine resource requirements
   b. Estimate activity durations
   c. Sequence activities
   d. Plan schedule management

182.

Which project approach entails near term work based upon high level assumptions and milestones, with risks and assumptions becoming more concrete as the project progresses? ***Select the best answer.***

   a. Lead roadmapping
   b. Rolling wave planning
   c. Cycle planning
   d. Proof of concept development

183.

_______________ involves pulling work from a backlog as resources become available. ***Select the best answer.***

    a. Backlog refinement
    b. Iterative scheduling
    c. Rolling wave planning
    d. On-demand scheduling

184.

Which statement describes the key benefit of the Plan Schedule Management process? ***Select the best answer.***

    a. It provides guidance and direction regarding how the project team can integrate new milestones into the project.
    b. It provides guidance and direction on how the project schedule will be managed throughout the project.
    c. It provides guidance and direction in architecting the various levels of the WBS.
    d. It provides guidance and direction in how to establish scheduling policies and procedures.

185.

The approach which describes using individuals with specialized knowledge or training is referred to as _______________. ***Select the best answer.***

    a. Brainstorming
    b. Delphi method
    c. Focus groups
    d. Exert judgement

186.

A data analysis technique which includes determining which schedule methodology to use, how to combine various methods on the project, how detailed the schedule needs to be, or the duration of waves for rolling wave planning is known as _______________. ***Select the best answer.***

    a. Alternative analysis
    b. Quantitative analysis
    c. Qualitative analysis
    d. Adaptive analysis

187.

As a component of the project management plan, the _____________ establishes the criteria and activities for developing, monitoring, and controlling the schedule. ***Select the best answer.***

    a. Schedule management plan
    b. Work package plan
    c. Milestone list
    d. Gantt chart

Elements of a schedule management plan include all of the following, except which items? *Select the best answer.*

a. Baseline EVM techniques
b. Rules for establishing percent complete
c. Schedule performance measurements
d. WBS activities

Work packages are the smallest unit of work that a project can be broken down to when creating the_____________. *Select the best answer.*

a. Work Breakdown Structure
b. Project plan
c. Schedule
d. Resource plan

As project manager for a leading mobile application developer, you have been requested by your Executive Sponsor to create a project schedule and identify project milestones. When identifying the milestones, which action should you do to indicate the period of time associated with the milestone? *Select the best answer.*

a. Display milestones as having zero duration, because they represent a significant point or event.
b. Display milestones as having a one-day duration, because they represent a significant day on the schedule.
c. Display milestones as having negative duration, as they should not be represented via duration.
d. Display milestones as one-week duration, as all milestones will result in at least one-week downtime to the project.

Which of the following is not a process within Project Cost Management? *Select the best answer.*

a. Estimate costs
b. Determine budget
c. Control costs
d. Develop cost baseline

As project manager for XYZ Kites, LLC you are midway through the project and evaluating progress to date. Your project Sponsor has scheduled a meeting with you to discuss the status of the project, and you need to propose a solution regarding schedule activity re-evaluation, if applicable. At the beginning of the project, you proposed adding a 2-week buffer to the schedule, in case some activities slipped beyond the expected finish dates. In evaluating the schedule variance, you notice the amount of earned schedule is 125 days while actual time 119 days, what should you advise the project Sponsor? *Select the best answer.*

a. The project is on schedule, but you will speak with the project team to determine if they can expedite a few activities to complete the project ahead of schedule.
b. The project is behind schedule, but you added a 2-week buffer to the project plan at the beginning of the project, so you should still be able to make the target due date.
c. The project is behind schedule; therefore, you will work with the project team to determine which activities can be accelerated to ensure meeting the project's due date.
d. The project is ahead of schedule; therefore, no activities need to be evaluated.

193.

Which of the following statements is true regarding cost estimates for agile projects? *Select the best answer.*

a. Agile projects should employ detailed cost estimation methods to generate low-level forecasts of labor costs.
b. Agile project may not benefit from detailed cost calculations due to frequent changes.
c. Agile projects can use lightweight estimation methods to generate fast forecasts of labor costs.
d. Agile projects can use flexible budgets, and adjust scope and schedule, as applicable, to stay within cost constraints.

194.

Which factor below is not an enterprise environmental factor that can influence Plan Cost Management? *Select the best answer.*

a. Currency exchange rates
b. Organizational culture
c. Market conditions
d. Financial controls

195.

Which of the following tools is not an organizational process asset of Plan Cost Management? *Select the best answer.*

a. Financial databases
b. Cost estimating and budgeting-related policies and guidelines
c. Historical information and lessons learned repository
d. Organizational structure

196.

Cost management processes are documented in the ________________? *Select the best answer.*

a. Budget
b. Cost management plan
c. Project plan
d. Financial database

197.

The project manager can stipulate in the cost management plan the degree to which cost estimates will be rounded up or down scope and project magnitude. This practice is referred to as which type of measure? *Select the best answer.*

   a.   Unit of measure
   b.   Productivity metric
   c.   Level of precision
   d.   Level of accuracy

198.

Which statement describes the key benefit of the estimate costs process? *Select the best answer.*

   a.   It determines the monetary resources required for the project.
   b.   It establishes the project budget.
   c.   It defines the currency conversion rates for projects with global resources.
   d.   It controls changes to the cost baseline.

199.

A cost estimate is a ____________ assessment of the likely costs for resources required to complete the activity. *Select the best answer.*

   a.   Rough guess
   b.   Qualitative
   c.   Quantitative
   d.   Comprehensive

200.

You work as a project manager for Do Lit, LLC, and you have scheduled a meeting with Accounting to discuss the project budget. Since you completed a project last year with comparable scope, budget, and duration to your current project, you could propose which cost estimating technique to determine project cost for the current assignment? *Select the best answer.*

   a.   Bottom-up estimating
   b.   Parametric estimating
   c.   Analogous estimating
   d.   Expert judgement

Notes:

1. *PMBOK© Guide* page numbers given on the following pages refer to the *PMBOK© Guide* pagination at the bottom of the page.
2. To validate the references, refer to *PMBOK© Guide©*. Non-members will need to purchase the *PMBOK© Guide©* or obtain membership to PMI.

ANSWER: D
Reference: PMBOK Guide 6th Edition, page 398 (Part 1 – Guide, Section 11)

ANSWER: B
Reference: PMBOK Guide 6th Edition, page 15 (Agile Practice Guide, Section 2)

ANSWER: B
Reference: PMBOK Guide 6th Edition, page 9 (Agile Practice Guide, Section 2)

ANSWER: A
Reference: PMBOK Guide 6th Edition, page 12 (Agile Practice Guide, Section 2)

ANSWER: C
Reference: PMBOK Guide 6th Edition, page 9 (Agile Practice Guide, Section 2)

ANSWER: D
Reference: PMBOK Guide 6th Edition, page 93 (Agile Practice Guide, Annex A1)

ANSWER: D
Reference: PMBOK Guide 6th Edition, page 40 (Agile Practice Guide, Section, 4)

ANSWER: B
Reference: PMBOK Guide 6th Edition, page 12 (Agile Practice Guide, Section 2)

ANSWER: A
Reference: PMBOK Guide 6th Edition, page 13 (Agile Practice Guide, Section 2)

ANSWER: C
Reference: PMBOK Guide 6th Edition, page 14 (Agile Practice Guide, Section 2)

ANSWER: B
Reference: PMBOK Guide 6th Edition, page 395 (Part 1 – Guide, Section 11)

ANSWER: D
Reference: PMBOK Guide 6th Edition, page 405 (Part 1 – Guide, Section 11)

13. CONCEPT: Risk Management (Risk Report)
ANSWER: B
Reference: PMBOK Guide 6th Edition, page 418 (Part 1 – Guide, Section 11)

14. CONCEPT: Risk Management (Risk Planning Process)
ANSWER: B
Reference: PMBOK Guide 6th Edition, page 402 (Part 1 – Guide, Section 11)

15. CONCEPT: Agile Principles (Lean/Kanban)
ANSWER: A
Reference: PMBOK Guide 6th Edition, page 14 (Agile Practice Guide, Section 2)

16. CONCEPT: Agile Principles (Lean/Kanban)
ANSWER: A
Reference: PMBOK Guide 6th Edition, page 17 (Agile Practice Guide, Section 3)

17. CONCEPT: Agile Principles (Lean/Kanban)
ANSWER: B
Reference: PMBOK Guide 6th Edition, page 17 (Agile Practice Guide, Section 3)

18. CONCEPT: Agile Principles (Lean/Kanban)
ANSWER: C
Reference: PMBOK Guide 6th Edition, page 17 (Agile Practice Guide, Section 3)

19. CONCEPT: Agile Principles (Lean/Kanban)
ANSWER: D
Reference: PMBOK Guide 6th Edition, page 17 (Agile Practice Guide, Section 3)

20. CONCEPT: Agile Principles (Lean/Kanban)
ANSWER: D
Reference: PMBOK Guide 6th Edition, page 17 (Agile Practice Guide, Section 3)

21. CONCEPT: Agile Principles (Lean/Kanban)
ANSWER: A
Reference: PMBOK Guide 6th Edition, page 20 (Agile Practice Guide, Section 3)

22. CONCEPT: Agile Principles (Lean/Kanban)
ANSWER: B
Reference: PMBOK Guide 6th Edition, page 20 (Agile Practice Guide, Section 3)

23. CONCEPT: Agile Principles (Lean/Kanban)
ANSWER: B
Reference: PMBOK Guide 6th Edition, page 21 (Agile Practice Guide, Section 3)

24. CONCEPT: Agile Principles (Lean/Kanban)
ANSWER: A
Reference: PMBOK Guide 6th Edition, page 22 (Agile Practice Guide, Section 3)

ANSWER: A
Reference: PMBOK Guide 6th Edition, page 25 (Agile Practice Guide, Section 3)

ANSWER: B
Reference: PMBOK Guide 6th Edition, page 24 (Agile Practice Guide, Section 3)

ANSWER: B
Reference: PMBOK Guide 6th Edition, page 24 (Agile Practice Guide, Section 3)

ANSWER: B
Reference: PMBOK Guide 6th Edition, page 24 (Agile Practice Guide, Section 3)

ANSWER: D
Reference: PMBOK Guide 6th Edition, page 24 (Agile Practice Guide, Section 3)

ANSWER: B
Reference: PMBOK Guide 6th Edition, page 24 (Agile Practice Guide, Section 3)

ANSWER: B
Reference: PMBOK Guide 6th Edition, page 15 (Agile Practice Guide, Section 2)

ANSWER: C
Reference: PMBOK Guide 6th Edition, page 15 (Agile Practice Guide, Section 2)

ANSWER: D
Reference: PMBOK Guide 6th Edition, page 15 (Agile Practice Guide, Section 2)

ANSWER: A
Reference: PMBOK Guide 6th Edition, page 15 (Agile Practice Guide, Section 2)

ANSWER: C
Reference: PMBOK Guide 6th Edition, page 15 (Agile Practice Guide, Section 2)

ANSWER: B
Reference: PMBOK Guide 6th Edition, page 15 (Agile Practice Guide, Section 2)

37. <u>CONCEPT: Agile Principles (Lean/Kanban)</u>
ANSWER: A
Reference: PMBOK Guide 6 Edition, page 15 (Agile Practice Guide, Section 2)

38. <u>CONCEPT: Agile Principles (Lean/Kanban)</u>
ANSWER: B
Reference: PMBOK Guide 6th Edition, page 16 (Agile Practice Guide, Section 2)

39. <u>CONCEPT: Agile Principles (Lean/Kanban)</u>
ANSWER: B
Reference: PMBOK Guide 6th Edition, page 9 (Agile Practice Guide, Section 2)

40. <u>CONCEPT: Agile Principles (Lean/Kanban)</u>
ANSWER: A
Reference: PMBOK Guide 6th Edition, page 14 (Agile Practice Guide, Section 2)

41. <u>CONCEPT: Agile Principles (Project Life Cycle)</u>
ANSWER: A
Reference: PMBOK Guide 6th Edition, page 18 (Agile Practice Guide, Section 3)

42. <u>CONCEPT: Agile Principles (Project Life Cycle)</u>
ANSWER: B
Reference: PMBOK Guide 6th Edition, page 18 (Agile Practice Guide, Section 3)

43. <u>CONCEPT: Agile Principles (Project Life Cycle)</u>
ANSWER: C
Reference: PMBOK Guide 6th Edition, page 18 (Agile Practice Guide, Section 3)

44. <u>CONCEPT: Agile Principles (Project Life Cycle)</u>
ANSWER: C
Reference: PMBOK Guide 6th Edition, page 18 (Agile Practice Guide, Section 3)

45. <u>CONCEPT: Agile Principles (Project Life Cycle)</u>
ANSWER: C
Reference: PMBOK Guide 6th Edition, page 18 (Agile Practice Guide, Section 3)

46. <u>CONCEPT: Agile Principles (Project Life Cycle)</u>
ANSWER: A
Reference: PMBOK Guide 6th Edition, page 18 (Agile Practice Guide, Section 3)

47. <u>CONCEPT: Agile Principles (Project Life Cycle)</u>
ANSWER: A
Reference: PMBOK Guide 6th Edition, page 18 (Agile Practice Guide, Section 3)

48. <u>CONCEPT: Agile Principles (Project Life Cycle)</u>
ANSWER: C
Reference: PMBOK Guide 6th Edition, page 20 (Agile Practice Guide, Section 3)

ANSWER: C
Reference: PMBOK Guide 6th Edition, page 20 (Agile Practice Guide, Section 3)

ANSWER: A
Reference: PMBOK Guide 6th Edition, page 20 (Agile Practice Guide, Section 3)

ANSWER: C
Reference: PMBOK Guide 6th Edition, page 20 (Agile Practice Guide, Section 3)

ANSWER: B
Reference: PMBOK Guide 6th Edition, page 21 (Agile Practice Guide, Section 3)

ANSWER: D
Reference: PMBOK Guide 6th Edition, page 21 (Agile Practice Guide, Section 3)

ANSWER: B
Reference: PMBOK Guide 6th Edition, page 25 (Agile Practice Guide, Section 3)

ANSWER: A
Reference: PMBOK Guide 6th Edition, page 25 (Agile Practice Guide, Section 3)

ANSWER: D
Reference: PMBOK Guide 6th Edition, page 21 (Agile Practice Guide, Section 3)

ANSWER: A
Reference: PMBOK Guide 6th Edition, page 25 (Agile Practice Guide, Section 3)

ANSWER: B
Reference: PMBOK Guide 6th Edition, page 25 (Agile Practice Guide, Section 3)

ANSWER: A
Reference: PMBOK Guide 6th Edition, page 25 (Agile Practice Guide, Section 3)

ANSWER: C
Reference: PMBOK Guide 6th Edition, page 9 (Agile Practice Guide, Section 2)

61.
ANSWER: B
Reference: PMBOK Guide 6th Edition, page 23 (Agile Practice Guide, Section 3)

62.
ANSWER: C
Reference: PMBOK Guide 6th Edition, page 22 (Agile Practice Guide, Section 3)

63.
ANSWER: D
Reference: PMBOK Guide 6th Edition, page 32 (Part 1 – Guide, Section 1)

$$NPV = -C_0 + \frac{C_1}{1+r} + \frac{C_2}{(1+r)^2} + \ldots + \frac{C_T}{(1+r)^T}$$

64.
ANSWER: C
Reference: PMBOK Guide 6th Edition, page 22 (Agile Practice Guide, Section 3; Webster's Dictionary)

65.
ANSWER: C
Reference: PMBOK Guide 6th Edition, page 23 (Agile Practice Guide, Section 3)

66.
ANSWER: C
Reference: PMBOK Guide 6th Edition, page 23 (Agile Practice Guide, Section 3)

67.
ANSWER: D
Reference: PMBOK Guide 6th Edition, page 21 (Agile Practice Guide, Section 3)

68.
ANSWER: D
Reference: PMBOK Guide 6th Edition, page 9 (Agile Practice Guide, Section 2)

69.
ANSWER: B
Reference: PMBOK Guide 6th Edition, page 12 (Agile Practice Guide, Section 2)

70.
ANSWER: D
Reference: PMBOK Guide 6th Edition, page 25 (Agile Practice Guide, Section 3)

71.
ANSWER: A
Reference: PMBOK Guide 6th Edition, page 26 (Agile Practice Guide, Section 3)

ANSWER: A
Reference: PMBOK Guide 6th Edition, page 26 (Agile Practice Guide, Section 3)

ANSWER: B
Reference: PMBOK Guide 6th Edition, page 27 (Agile Practice Guide, Section 3)

ANSWER: A
Reference: PMBOK Guide 6th Edition, page 27 (Agile Practice Guide, Section 3)

ANSWER: B
Reference: PMBOK Guide 6th Edition, page 27 (Agile Practice Guide, Section 3)

ANSWER: A
Reference: PMBOK Guide 6th Edition, page 27 (Agile Practice Guide, Section 3)

ANSWER: C
Reference: PMBOK Guide 6th Edition, page 51 (Agile Practice Guide, Section 5)

ANSWER: D
Reference: PMBOK Guide 6th Edition, page 51 (Agile Practice Guide, Section 5)

ANSWER: D
Reference: PMBOK Guide 6th Edition, page 27 (Agile Practice Guide, Section 3)

ANSWER: B
Reference: PMBOK Guide 6th Edition, page 51 (Agile Practice Guide, Section 5)

ANSWER: D
Reference: PMBOK Guide 6th Edition, page 27 (Agile Practice Guide, Section 3)

ANSWER: A
Reference: PMBOK Guide 6th Edition, page 28 (Agile Practice Guide, Section 3)

ANSWER: B
Reference: PMBOK Guide 6th Edition, page 28 (Agile Practice Guide, Section 3)

84. CONCEPT: Agile Principles (Project Life Cycle)
ANSWER: B
Reference: PMBOK Guide 6th Edition, page 28 (Agile Practice Guide, Section 3)

85. CONCEPT: Agile Principles (Lean/Kanban)
ANSWER: B
Reference: PMBOK Guide 6th Edition, page 31 (Agile Practice Guide, Section 3)

86. CONCEPT: Agile Principles (Agile Routines) 1
ANSWER: A
Reference: PMBOK Guide 6th Edition, page 33 (Agile Practice Guide, Section 4)

87. CONCEPT: Agile Principles (Agile Teams)
ANSWER: D
Reference: PMBOK Guide 6th Edition, page 33 (Agile Practice Guide, Section 4)

88. CONCEPT: Agile Principles (Agile Teams)
ANSWER: B
Reference: PMBOK Guide 6th Edition, page 33 (Agile Practice Guide, Section 4)

89. CONCEPT: Agile Principles (Project Teams)
ANSWER: C
Reference: PMBOK Guide 6th Edition, page 34 (Agile Practice Guide, Section 4)

90. CONCEPT: Agile Principles (Project Teams) 5
ANSWER: A
Reference: PMBOK Guide 6th Edition, page 32 (Agile Practice Guide, Section 3)

91. CONCEPT: Project Standards (Planning Processes)
ANSWER: C
Reference: PMBOK Guide 6th Edition, page 565 (Part 2 - Guide, Section 3)

92. CONCEPT: Agile Principles (Project Teams)
ANSWER: D
Reference: PMBOK Guide 6th Edition, page 31 (Agile Practice Guide, Section 3)

93. CONCEPT: Agile Principles (Agile Approaches)
ANSWER: A
Reference: PMBOK Guide 6th Edition, page 32 (Agile Practice Guide, Section 3)

94. CONCEPT: Agile Principles (Agile Approaches)
ANSWER: D
Reference: PMBOK Guide 6th Edition, page 32 (Agile Practice Guide, Section 3)

95. CONCEPT: Agile Principles (Agile Teams)
ANSWER: C
Reference: PMBOK Guide 6th Edition, page 40 (Agile Practice Guide, Section 4)

96. CONCEPT: Agile Principles (Agile Teams)

ANSWER: D

Reference: PMBOK Guide 6th Edition, page 41 (Agile Practice Guide, Section 4)

97. CONCEPT: Agile Principles (Agile Teams)

ANSWER: A

Reference: PMBOK Guide 6th Edition, page 41 (Agile Practice Guide, Section 4)

98. CONCEPT: Agile Principles (Agile Teams)

ANSWER: C

Reference: PMBOK Guide 6th Edition, page 41 (Agile Practice Guide, Section 4)

99. CONCEPT: Agile Principles (Agile Teams)

ANSWER: B

Reference: PMBOK Guide 6th Edition, page 42 (Agile Practice Guide, Section 4)

100.   CONCEPT: Agile Principles (Agile Routines)

ANSWER: B

Reference: PMBOK Guide 6th Edition, page 50 (Agile Practice Guide, Section 5)

101.   CONCEPT: Agile Principles (Present Value)

ANSWER: C

Reference: PMBOK Guide 6th Edition, page 473 (Part 1 – Guide, Section 12)

$$PV = \frac{C}{(1 + i)^n}$$

102.   CONCEPT: Project Management (Agile Routines)

ANSWER: C

Reference: PMBOK Guide 6th Edition, page 46 (Agile Practice Guide, Section 4)

103.   CONCEPT: Agile Principles (Agile Routines)

ANSWER: B

Reference: PMBOK Guide 6th Edition, page 46 (Agile Practice Guide, Section 4)

104.   CONCEPT: Agile Principles (Agile Teams)

ANSWER: A

Reference: PMBOK Guide 6th Edition, page 47 (Agile Practice Guide, Section 4)

105.   CONCEPT: Agile Principles (Agile Teams) 20

ANSWER: C

Reference: PMBOK Guide 6th Edition, page 47 (Agile Practice Guide, Section 4)

106.   CONCEPT: Agile Principles (Agile Teams)

ANSWER: B

Reference: PMBOK Guide 6th Edition, page 49 (Agile Practice Guide, Section 5)

107.   CONCEPT: Agile Principles (Agile Teams)
ANSWER: D
Reference: PMBOK Guide 6th Edition, page 50 (Agile Practice Guide, Section 5)

108.   CONCEPT: Agile Principles (Agile Teams)
ANSWER: A
Reference: PMBOK Guide 6th Edition, page 49 (Agile Practice Guide, Section 5)

109.   CONCEPT: Agile Principles (Agile Routines)
ANSWER: C
Reference: PMBOK Guide 6th Edition, page 52 (Agile Practice Guide, Section 5)

110.   CONCEPT: Agile Principles (Agile Routines)
ANSWER: C
Reference: PMBOK Guide 6th Edition, page 52 (Agile Practice Guide, Section 5)

111.   CONCEPT: Agile Principles (Project Life Cycle)
ANSWER: C
Reference: PMBOK Guide 6th Edition, page 52 (Agile Practice Guide, Section 5)

112.   CONCEPT: Agile Principles (Agile Routines)
ANSWER: A
Reference: PMBOK Guide 6th Edition, page 52 (Agile Practice Guide, Section 5)

113.   CONCEPT: Agile Principles (Agile Routines)
ANSWER: B
Reference: PMBOK Guide 6th Edition, page 53 (Agile Practice Guide, Section 5)

114.   CONCEPT: Agile Principles (Agile Routines)
ANSWER: D
Reference: PMBOK Guide 6th Edition, page 54 (Agile Practice Guide, Section 5)

115.   CONCEPT: Agile Principles (Agile Routines)
ANSWER: B
Reference: PMBOK Guide 6th Edition, page 54 (Agile Practice Guide, Section 5)

116.   CONCEPT: Agile Principles (Agile Routines)
ANSWER: B
Reference: PMBOK Guide 6th Edition, page 55 (Agile Practice Guide, Section 5)

117.   CONCEPT: Agile Principles (Agile Routines)
ANSWER: D
Reference: PMBOK Guide 6th Edition, page 52 (Agile Practice Guide, Section 5)

118.   CONCEPT: Agile Principles (Agile Routines)
ANSWER: B
Reference: PMBOK Guide 6th Edition, page 56 (Agile Practice Guide, Section 5)

119.   CONCEPT: Agile Principles (Project Routines)

ANSWER: D

Reference: PMBOK Guide 6th Edition, page 56 (Agile Practice Guide, Section 5)

120.   CONCEPT: Agile Principles (Project Routines)

ANSWER: A

Reference: PMBOK Guide 6th Edition, page 56 (Agile Practice Guide, Section 5)

121.   CONCEPT: Agile Principles (Project Routines)

ANSWER: A

Reference: PMBOK Guide 6th Edition, page 56 (Agile Practice Guide, Section 5)

122.   CONCEPT: Agile Principles (Project Routines)

ANSWER: C

Reference: PMBOK Guide 6th Edition, page 56 (Agile Practice Guide, Section 5)

123.   CONCEPT: Agile Principles (Project Routines)

ANSWER: B

Reference: PMBOK Guide 6th Edition, page 57 (Agile Practice Guide, Section 5)

124.   CONCEPT: Agile Principles (Agile Routines)

ANSWER: B

Reference: PMBOK Guide 6th Edition, page 58 (Agile Practice Guide, Section 5)

125.   CONCEPT: Agile Principles (Project Metrics)

ANSWER: C

Reference: PMBOK Guide 6th Edition, page 60 (Agile Practice Guide, Section 5)

126.   CONCEPT: Agile Principles (Project Metrics)

ANSWER: D

Reference: PMBOK Guide 6th Edition, page 60 (Agile Practice Guide, Section 5)

127.   CONCEPT: Agile Principles (Project Metrics)

ANSWER: C

Reference: PMBOK Guide 6th Edition, page 60 (Agile Practice Guide, Section 5)

128.   CONCEPT: Agile Principles (Project Metrics)

ANSWER: A

Reference: PMBOK Guide 6th Edition, page 61 (Agile Practice Guide, Section 5)

129.   CONCEPT: Agile Principles (Project Metrics)

ANSWER: B

Reference: PMBOK Guide 6th Edition, page 61 (Agile Practice Guide, Section 5)

130.   CONCEPT: Agile Principles (Project Metrics)

ANSWER: D

Reference: PMBOK Guide 6th Edition, page 61 (Agile Practice Guide, Section 5)

131.
ANSWER: A
Reference: PMBOK Guide 6th Edition, page 61 (Agile Practice Guide, Section 5)

132.
ANSWER: D
Reference: PMBOK Guide 6th Edition, page 62 (Agile Practice Guide, Section 5)

133.
ANSWER: C
Reference: PMBOK Guide 6th Edition, page 62 (Agile Practice Guide, Section 5)

134.
ANSWER: A
Reference: PMBOK Guide 6th Edition, page 62 (Agile Practice Guide, Section 5)

135.
ANSWER: B
Reference: PMBOK Guide 6th Edition, page 63 (Agile Practice Guide, Section 5)

136.
ANSWER: C
Reference: PMBOK Guide 6th Edition, page 63 (Agile Practice Guide, Section 5)

137.
ANSWER: B
Reference: PMBOK Guide 6th Edition, page 63 (Agile Practice Guide, Section 5)

138.
ANSWER: A
Reference: PMBOK Guide 6th Edition, page 55 (Agile Practice Guide, Section 5)

139.
ANSWER: B
Reference: PMBOK Guide 6th Edition, page 64 (Agile Practice Guide, Section 5)

140.
ANSWER: D
Reference: PMBOK Guide 6th Edition, page 64 (Agile Practice Guide, Section 5)

141.
ANSWER: C
Reference: PMBOK Guide 6th Edition, page 65 (Agile Practice Guide, Section 5)

142.
ANSWER: D
Reference: PMBOK Guide 6th Edition, page 65 (Agile Practice Guide, Section 5)

143.   CONCEPT: Agile Principles (Project Metrics)

ANSWER: A

Reference: PMBOK Guide 6th Edition, page 66 (Agile Practice Guide, Section 5)

144.   CONCEPT: Agile Principles (Project Metrics)

ANSWER: A

Reference: PMBOK Guide 6th Edition, page 66 (Agile Practice Guide, Section 5)

145.   CONCEPT: Agile Principles (Project Metrics)

ANSWER: C

Reference: PMBOK Guide 6th Edition, page 69 (Agile Practice Guide, Section 5)

146.   CONCEPT: Agile Principles (Project Metrics)

ANSWER: A

Reference: PMBOK Guide 6th Edition, page 69 (Agile Practice Guide, Section 5)

147.   CONCEPT: Agile Principles (Project Metrics)

ANSWER: C

Reference: PMBOK Guide 6th Edition, page 69 (Agile Practice Guide, Section 5)

148.   CONCEPT: Agile Principles (Project Metrics)

ANSWER: B

Reference: PMBOK Guide 6th Edition, page 69 (Agile Practice Guide, Section 5)

149.   CONCEPT: Agile Principles (Organizational Environments)

ANSWER: C

Reference: PMBOK Guide 6th Edition, page 82 (Agile Practice Guide, Section 6)

150.   CONCEPT: Agile Principles (Organizational Environments)

ANSWER: C

Reference: PMBOK Guide 6th Edition, page 82 (Agile Practice Guide, Section 6)

151.   CONCEPT: Agile Principles (Organizational Environments)

ANSWER: D

Reference: PMBOK Guide 6th Edition, page 73 (Agile Practice Guide, Section 6)

152.   CONCEPT: Agile Principles (Organizational Environments)

ANSWER: C

Reference: PMBOK Guide 6th Edition, page 75 (Agile Practice Guide, Section 6)

153.   CONCEPT: Agile Principles (Organizational Environments)

ANSWER: B

Reference: PMBOK Guide 6th Edition, page 75 (Agile Practice Guide, Section 6)

154.   CONCEPT: Agile Principles (Agile Teams)

ANSWER: D

Reference: PMBOK Guide 6th Edition, page 40 (Agile Practice Guide, Section 4)

155.
ANSWER: B

Reference: PMBOK Guide 6th Edition, page 40 (Agile Practice Guide, Section 4)

156.
ANSWER: A

Reference: PMBOK Guide 6th Edition, page 58 (Agile Practice Guide, Section 5)

157.
ANSWER: B

Reference: PMBOK Guide 6th Edition, page 58 (Agile Practice Guide, Section 5)

158.
ANSWER: D

Reference: PMBOK Guide 6th Edition, page 58 (Agile Practice Guide, Section 5)

159.
ANSWER: A

Reference: PMBOK Guide 6th Edition, page 78 (Agile Practice Guide, Section 6)

160.
ANSWER: A

Reference: PMBOK Guide 6th Edition, page 78 (Agile Practice Guide, Section 6)

161.
ANSWER: A

Reference: PMBOK Guide 6th Edition, page 39 (Agile Practice Guide, Section 6)

162.
ANSWER: A

Reference: PMBOK Guide 6th Edition, page 39 (Part 1 – Guide, Section 2)

163.
ANSWER: B

Reference: PMBOK Guide 6th Edition, page 52 (Part 1 – Guide, Section 3)

164.
ANSWER: C

Reference: PMBOK Guide 6th Edition, page 53 (Part 1 – Guide, Section 3)

165.
ANSWER: B

Reference: PMBOK Guide 6th Edition, page 56 (Part 1 – Guide, Section 3)

166.
ANSWER: D

Reference: PMBOK Guide 6th Edition, page 70 (Part 1 – Guide, Section 4)

167.   CONCEPT: PMBOK (Integration)

ANSWER: C

Reference: PMBOK Guide 6th Edition, page 72 (Part 1 – Guide, Section 4)

168.   CONCEPT: PMBOK (Integration)

ANSWER: C

Reference: PMBOK Guide 6th Edition, page 74 (Part 1 – Guide, Section 4)

169.   CONCEPT: PMBOK (Integration)

ANSWER: D

Reference: PMBOK Guide 6th Edition, page 74 (Part 1 – Guide, Section 4)

170.   CONCEPT: PMBOK (Integration)

ANSWER: A

Reference: PMBOK Guide 6th Edition, page 74 (Part 1 – Guide, Section 4)

171.   CONCEPT: PMBOK (Scope)

ANSWER: D

Reference: PMBOK Guide 6th Edition, page 129 (Part 1 – Guide, Section 5)

172.   CONCEPT: PMBOK (Scope)

ANSWER: A

Reference: PMBOK Guide 6th Edition, page 131 (Part 1 – Guide, Section 5)

173.   CONCEPT: PMBOK (Scope)

ANSWER: C

Reference: PMBOK Guide 6th Edition, page 131 (Part 1 – Guide, Section 5)

174.   CONCEPT: PMBOK (Scope)

ANSWER: B

Reference: PMBOK Guide 6th Edition, page 131 (Part 1 – Guide, Section 5)

175.   CONCEPT: PMBOK (Scope)

ANSWER: D

Reference: PMBOK Guide 6th Edition, page 133 (Part 1 – Guide, Section 5)

176.   CONCEPT: PMBOK (Scope)

ANSWER: D

Reference: PMBOK Guide 6th Edition, page 136 (Part 1 – Guide, Section 5)

177.   CONCEPT: PMBOK (Scope)

ANSWER: D

Reference: PMBOK Guide 6th Edition, page 137 (Part 1 – Guide, Section 5)

178.   CONCEPT: PMBOK (Scope)

ANSWER: D

Reference: PMBOK Guide 6th Edition, page 137 (Part 1 – Guide, Section 5)

ANSWER: A
Reference: PMBOK Guide 6th Edition, page 142 (Part 1 – Guide, Section 5)

ANSWER: D
Reference: PMBOK Guide 6th Edition, page 143 (Part 1 - Guide, Section 5)

ANSWER: A
Reference: PMBOK Guide 6th Edition, page 173 (Part 1 – Guide, Section 6)

ANSWER: B
Reference: PMBOK Guide 6th Edition, page 177 (Part 1 – Guide, Section 6)

ANSWER: D
Reference: PMBOK Guide 6th Edition, page 177 (Part 1 – Guide, Section 6)

ANSWER: B
Reference: PMBOK Guide 6th Edition, page 179 (Part 1 – Guide, Section 6)

ANSWER: D
Reference: PMBOK Guide 6th Edition, page 181 (Part 1 – Guide, Section 6)

ANSWER: A
Reference: PMBOK Guide 6th Edition, page 181 (Part 1 – Guide, Section 6)

ANSWER: A
Reference: PMBOK Guide 6th Edition, page 181 (Part 1 – Guide, Section 6)

ANSWER: D
Reference: PMBOK Guide 6th Edition, page 182 (Part 1 – Guide, Section 6)

ANSWER: A
Reference: PMBOK Guide 6th Edition, page 185 (Part 1 – Guide, Section 6)

ANSWER: A
Reference: PMBOK Guide 6th Edition, page 186 (Part 1 – Guide, Section 6)

ANSWER: D
Reference: PMBOK Guide 6th Edition, page 231 (Part 1 – Guide, Section 7)

ANSWER: D
Reference: PMBOK Guide 6th Edition, page 232 (Part 1 – Guide, Section 7)

ANSWER: C
Reference: PMBOK Guide 6th Edition, page 234 (Part 1 – Guide, Section 7)

ANSWER: D
Reference: PMBOK Guide 6th Edition, page 236 (Part 1 – Guide, Section 7)

ANSWER: D
Reference: PMBOK Guide 6th Edition, page 237 (Part 1 – Guide, Section 7)

ANSWER: B
Reference: PMBOK Guide 6th Edition, page 238 (Part 1 – Guide, Section 7)

ANSWER: C
Reference: PMBOK Guide 6th Edition, page 238 (Part 1 – Guide, Section 7)

ANSWER: A
Reference: PMBOK Guide 6th Edition, page 240 (Part 1 – Guide, Section 7)

ANSWER: C
Reference: PMBOK Guide 6th Edition, page 241(Part 1 – Guide, Section 7)

ANSWER: C
Reference: PMBOK Guide 6th Edition, page 244 (Part 1 – Guide, Section 7)

About the Author

Dr. Renay Carver, PhD, CISM, CRISC, PMP, SSBB, CSM, CSP, POPM, SAFe is an accomplished operations and technology strategist with over 20 years' experience leading diverse business teams and clients through transformational information security, risk and change strategic initiatives. As a skilled risk and cyber management practitioner, Dr. Carver has provided direct leadership executing cross-functional, large scale and complex business programs for multinational organizations. She conducts personal, group and corporate training for cyber security and risk professionals seeking guidance in implementing continuity and security solutions to address compliance and strategic needs. In addition to a PhD in Industrial/Organizational Psychology, Dr. Carver holds an MBA (Marketing) and an MS (Finance) degree.